Cover Photo:

The kitchen of a Southern Railway dining car circa 1920. Southern Railway publicity photo, author's collection.

CONTENTS

Prelude………………………………………………………..4

Introduction…………………………………………………..8

General Instructions & Notes for Service……………..…10

Beverages……………………………………………………14

Breads………………………………………………………..15

Cereals………………………………………………………..22

Desserts……………………………………………..………..23

When Train Tickets Were Money………………………….…34

Eggs…………………………………………………………..35

Fowl…………………………………………………………..37

The First Railroad in the South……………………………...43

Fruits…………………………………………………………44

Juices…………………………………………………………46

Meats…………………………………………………………47

Omelets………………………………………………………65

Relishes a la Carte…………………………………………..67

Relishes Table D'Hote……………………………………...68

Salads a la Carte…………………………………………….69

Salads Table D'Hote………………………………………..71

Sandwiches……………………………………………..74

Sauces…………………………………………………77

Seafood..………………………………………………80

Soups…………………………………………………..85

Vegetables……………………………………………..90

PRELUDE: A BRIEF HISTORY OF THE DINING CAR

A railroad dining car is a demonstration of efficiency. The meals that railroads were famous for came out of a kitchen measuring seven feet wide and twenty feet long. In that confined space, a chef and two or three assistants, worked without getting in each other's way while rolling down the track at speeds up to 80 mph. But it wasn't always that way.

Railroads began crossing the country in the 1830's. Locomotives were small, with a range of only a hundred miles or so. Division points were established at these spots where an engine could be serviced and refueled for the return trip to its home terminal. These service stops usually lasted only 20 minutes—the time necessary to service or change locomotives. In those early days, it was a mad dash for passengers to eat. The railroads weren't concerned about the quality of the food or the service. They thought their business was transportation, not food. There were many complaints from passengers about often only being able to get a bite or two before having to run back to the train. Such complaints fell on deaf ears, which was probably a good thing. There is some anecdotal evidence to suggest that some of these trackside eateries "boosted" their profit margin by "touching up" the uneaten portions and serving them to the passengers on the next train. There are no records of illness or death occurring from such practices, probably due to the minimal amount of food that a person could consume at a stop. The other catch was that the customers had to pay in advance.

Any economist will tell you this was the result of a monopoly—high prices and poor quality.

Dining cars began appearing on trains shortly after the Civil War. George Pullman had developed the sleeping car, locomotives were becoming larger, could travel farther, and the need for frequent service stops was diminishing. Although there were many "one off" experiments with food service on a moving train, often little more than a converted baggage car with a cast iron stove on one end and tables made from long planks of wood for the guests to sit at filling the rest of the car, it is generally accepted that Pullman manufactured the first true dining car in 1868, naming it Delmonico after the Swiss-born New York restaurateur.

It still took some time for the dining car to be accepted by railroad management. Diners were expensive to maintain and operate. The typical crew consisted of a steward who was in charge of the car and its crew, a chef and two or three assistants, and four to six waiters. The "modern" dining car that most people who traveled by train in the pre-Amtrak era remember, was developed between 1900 and 1910. It consisted of an enclosed kitchen with overhead water tanks. Hot water was obtained by running the water through a boiler in the firebox of the coal fired oven. Seating capacity was 36. There were 12 tables in the car. Along one side each table seated four, while the other side had tables seating two. Later the capacity was increased to 48 by replacing the tables for two with tables for four. Still, with a typical train carrying as many as 300 passengers, eight to ten seatings would often be required for each meal.

Dining cars never made money. The economics of operating a fully equipped 36 to 48 seat restaurant with a captive market [those passengers on the train] made turning a profit impossible. The industry average was each dollar of revenue cost $1.38 to produce.

By the 1920's there was virtually nothing to distinguish the service of any railroads serving points A and B. For the economy minded, there was coach service while Pullman service was available if you desired to travel First Class.

The marketing departments then turned to the one thing that could differentiate them from the competition—food service. While the Santa Fe promoted their "Meals by Fred Harvey", most lines had to create a specialty item such as the Northern Pacific's "Big Baked Potato" which was required to be blemish free and weigh a minimum of one pound, or the Southern Railway's "Fried Chicken, Southern Style, Cream Gravy".

Electrical operation of the stove and oven wasn't an option at this time because the locomotives were still steam powered. Even when diesel-electric locomotives came into wide use [after WW2], the dining cars still relied on coal fired stoves and ovens. Economics played a role in this. Once the war ended, the automobile and aircraft were gaining in popularity as means of travel with trains losing passengers to both. So passenger diesels were equipped with steam generators, basically a boiler, to provide steam for heating the passenger cars in the winter months.

One of the traditions of dining cars is that the customer would write their own order on the meal check. There are two explanations given for this practice. The first had to do with the literacy of the waiters. They tended to be Negro, and therefore were more likely to be illiterate, although jobs with the railroads made them some of the best paid members of their communities. The second explanation is that, given the motion that a dining car undergoes as it rolls down the tracks, it was easier to write the ticket on the table, and it was more practical for the diner to do it themselves than to have the waiter lean over, write the ticket and block the aisle in the process.

Outside of car construction, the dining car remained remarkably resilient to change. A chef from Pullman's Delmonico would have been right at home on a 1970's Amtrak diner. Instead of ice, dry ice would be the chosen method of refrigeration and Presto Logs [compressed sawdust] would have replaced the coal bucket and scoop for firing the stove and oven.

Amtrak took over the operation of intercity passenger trains on May 1, 1971. Steam lines varied in location on passenger cars from railroad to railroad, and various railroads had different, battery powered electrical systems for the passenger cars. The smorgasbord of equipment which Amtrak inherited from the various railroads led to the effort to standardize. The demise of the coal stove can be traced to the bitterly cold winter of 1981. Steam lines froze on nearly all trains, resulting in no heat in the passenger cars. The literal avalanche of complaints forced Amtrak's hand, and steam heat was eliminated in 1982. Simultaneous with that, the decision was made to convert the dining cars to all electric operation, bringing the demise of the Presto Log and dry ice cooled refrigerators.

What you have here is a tribute to the men who made "dinner in the diner" such a memorable experience, and to their talent. Cooking in a coal-fired oven required a great deal of education and skill, especially when the kitchen is traveling at interstate highway speeds. While you won't find any exotic fare here, you will find good meals that are hearty, filling, and easy to prepare in your home kitchen.

Introduction

This cookbook has been reproduced from original documents obtained from various archives throughout the area served by the Southern Railway [now part of Norfolk Southern Corporation]. They also date from a time when the effects of healthy eating weren't as well known as they are now. You will find copious amounts of lard and other fats.

This book recalls a time when individual railroads operated their own passenger trains and the food they served in their dining cars reflected the traditional foods from the regions they served.

A meal served in a railroad dining car was an experience like no other. The starched linen tablecloth, fine silver and china, the fresh flower in the vase by the window and, most important, what was outside that window—the ever changing American landscape.

Gordon Mooneyhan
Myrtle Beach, SC
2013

General Instructions and Notes for Service

What was so special about a meal in a dining car? Attention to detail for one thing. Graham Claytor, Jr., Southern Railway President from 1966 to 1977, and later, President of Amtrak, once told me the worst thing a railroad could do was to serve a bad cup of coffee in their dining car. His reasoning was you didn't know whom you were serving. If the person was one of your shippers, bad service might cause him to route his freight over a competitor's line. This attention to detail goes back even farther. The following is a memo from E.L. Frapart, Superintendent of Dining Cars for the Southern Railway, dated in the early 1950's.

REGULAR AND CRESCENT SERVICE

For breakfast, chef cooks should use utmost discretion in the advance preparation of breakfast items, such as bacon and sausage. These items, where possible should be cooked to order; however, on heavy lines it will be necessary to prepare a limited amount in advance. Toast must be made as ordered. Also at lunch and dinner, cooks must use extreme care and not prepare too much food in advance.

There is a charge of 50¢ per person for service outside of dining car and you will note what joint circular letter dated January 11, 1951, addressed to all Dining Car Stewards has to say about service outside of dining car.

If any person desires a double portion of any kind of juice, you will serve a water tumbler full, and the price will be 60¢.

When tomato catsup and chili sauce are opened, they then must be kept under refrigeration.

NOTES FOR SERVICE

Waiters, when serving the meal, should inquire of patron if condiments are desired. Waiters will also inquire if coffee is to be served with the meal or later.

All waiters, when serving roast beef or steak, must serve serrated blade steak knife.

When new menus are issued, all employees will acquaint themselves with the service of the items appearing on the menu.

The coffee must be made by the chef cook. Fill the coffee measure with hot water and put on range until water boils, then put one [1] package of coffee in the water. Stir this coffee with a spoon until it dissolves, then pour into coffee urn and pull coffee through urn three [3] times. The urn must be washed out each trip with baking soda and when pulling the water and baking soda through the urn, work the valve in order to get any sediments that may be in the valve.

At the beginning of each trip, the chef cook will see that the top of the range is swept off and that the soot boxes at the bottom of the range are cleaned out thoroughly.

E.L. Frapart,
Superintendent, Dining Cars

Notice the reference to soot boxes? These dining cars had coal-fired stoves and ovens. So, in addition to the crowded space for three cooks [approximately 7 feet by 15 feet], they had to also deal with cooking without conventional temperature controls. The net result was a hot kitchen in the winter; and even hotter in the summer. In some instances, a temperature is given in brackets []. This comes from my trial and error in preparing some of these delicious meals.

Passenger services in general, and dining cars in particular, have never been profitable for railroads. Even though passengers are, in effect, self-loading and unloading, they do demand a certain degree of comfort. Those needs led to specialized equipment, i.e. coaches, sleeping cars and dining cars, and this equipment was a compromise between comfort and getting the maximum number of people into the given space.

Another memo from Mr. Frapart concerns cream:

Atlanta, GA., July 10, 1952

ALL DINING CAR STEWARDS, CHEF COOKS, AND PANTRYMEN:

I have information that pitchers of cream are allowed to stay on the tables during the entire service of a meal whether any passengers are seated at the table or not.

You will please see that all waiters keep cream off the tables except when service is being performed which requires cream.

E.L. Frapart
Superintendent,
Dining Cars

This memo was copied to about a dozen other individuals involved with the dining car operations. Why the concern over cream? It was an area where they could control the expense. Servings on dining cars tended to be on the generous side. And it wasn't limited to the Southern. The following is a recipe from the Pennsylvania Railroad for their PRR Salad Bowl:

¼ head crisp lettuce [core removed, leaves pulled apart]
1 good size ripe tomato [cut into eight [8] portions]
2 green onions or scallions
¼ cucumber
3 radishes
1 stalk celery
¾ ounce Roquefort cheese

How many servings would that yield? On the PRR, one. It is simply an extension of Graham Claytor's philosophy. You never know who you will be serving, so make sure it's a: good, and b: plentiful. The end result of this philosophy was meal costs that were higher than could reasonably be recovered. Extreme? Possibly…but it's one of the reasons that travel by train was, and still is, so enjoyable.

Another thing to notice is these recipes are really good, healthy fare. You won't find exotic quiches in here. Food preparation had to be easy and simple, especially when the kitchen was rolling down the tracks at 80 miles an hour!

The Southern Railway cookbook was never really a book. Rather, it was a collection of mimeographed pages that were kept in either a manila folder or large envelope in each dining car. While this made it easy to change recipes [in effect, you had a larger version of the family recipe box], it also means that this record may not be complete. The primary source was an original cookbook that came from a Southern Railway dining car. Additional recipes were subsequently discovered in archives of several historical societies in the area served by the Southern. Because of this, I cannot say this record is complete. It is, however, the most complete record of Southern Railway recipes published to date.

As you read through this collection, you may notice that some of the recipes seem to "skip" certain steps, e.g. in the Southern Corn Cakes, after the ingredients, the directions say to thin to a batter with milk. It is assumed that you know to cook them in a lightly greased skillet.

BEVERAGES

COCOA: Pot—serve cup and saucer, 1 cocoa pot full of cocoa made with sweet milk.

COFFEE: Pot—serve cup and saucer, 1 coffeepot full of coffee and pitcher of cream.

ICED TEA: Pot of boiling water with tea bag in same. Serve a glass of ice, underlined with a fruit saucer, ¼ lemon in fruit saucer side of ice tea glass. On Table D' Hote, serve iced tea in glass. Ice teaspoon for service.

MILK: Serve in original container or bottle. Waiter should pour milk from container at table, in presence of guest, into water glass.

POSTUM: Pot—serve two individual packages or containers of postum, underlined with fruit saucer; cup and saucer and hot water pot full of boiling water. Pitcher of cream.

SANKA: Pot—serve two individual packages of Instant Sanka in fruit saucer. Cup and saucer and hot water pot full of boiling water. Pitcher of cream.

HOT TEA: Pot—serve cup and saucer, tea bag in fruit saucer on side. Tea pot full of boiling water. Waiter should ask guest whether lemon or cream is desired. Serve 2 slices of lemon in fruit saucer or pitcher of cream.

What's postum? It's a coffee substitute that was developed during WW2 made from grain. The war saw many items rationed in the United States. Coffee was just one of many.

BREADS

BRAN MUFFINS: Serve 3 bran muffins on A La Carte, 2 bran muffins on Club Breakfast, on tea plate underlined with a doily. Number 45 ramekin of marmalade or preserves on B&B plate with pat of butter.

4 tablespoons shortening
½ cup sugar
2 eggs   2 cups
all-bran
1½ cups milk   2 cups
sifted flour
1 teaspoon salt
5 teaspoons baking powder

PREPARATION: Cream shortening and sugar thoroughly, add eggs, beat well, then stir in all-bran and milk and let soak until most of the moisture is taken up. Sift flour, salt, and baking powder and add to the first mixture, and stir only until the flour disappears. Fill greased muffin pan 2/3 full and bake in a moderately hot oven 25-30 minutes. NOTE: When sour milk or buttermilk is used instead of sweet milk, reduce baking powder to 2 teaspoons and add 1 teaspoon soda. NOTE: WHEN BAKING HOT MUFFINS BAKE A SMALL AMOUNT AT A TIME SO THAT YOU WILL BE ABLE TO SERVE THE MUFFINS HOT.

BUTTERED TOAST: Serve same as dry toast with melted butter spread over toast. Preparation same as for dry toast.

CORN DODGERS:

2 eggs   ½
teaspoon sugar
½ cup corn meal   pinch
salt
2 cups flour   canned
cream
1 heaping tablespoon baking powder

Mix all ingredients together. Drop tablespoons of batter into hot oil and deep fry until golden brown.

DRY TOAST: 3 slices A La Carte or 2 slices Club Breakfast on tea plate underlined with a doily. Number 45 ramekin of marmalade or preserves on B&B plate with pat of butter. Butter should be placed on B&B plate with a fork; never with the fingers as finger marks show very plainly on a pat of butter. Crust to be trimmed from bread, and bread cut diagonally.

PREPARATION: Toast for all purposes should be prepared in the oven rather than on the broiler. The bread may be placed in a biscuit pan, then placed in the oven to bring about the desired results.
NOTE: WHEN PREPARING TOAST, MAKE A SMALL AMOUNT AT A TIME SO THAT YOU WILL BE ABLE TO SERVE THE TOAST HOT.

FLAKE CRACKERS: Serve 4 double flake crackers on tea plate underlined with a doily, or 2 individual packages of crackers on tea plate underlined with a doily.

HOT CORN BREAD: Serve two 3-inch squares of corn bread on tea plate underlined with a paper doily for A La Carte. Serve one 3-inch square for Table d'hôte. Pat of butter on B&B plate.

3¼ cups corn meal	4 cups
milk	
1 teaspoon salt	3 eggs
3 teaspoons baking powder	
1-cup lard	

Mix corn meal, salt, milk, and eggs together thoroughly, then add lard and baking powder. Grease pan and cook in a hot oven. Bread to be about ½-inch thick. NOTE: WHEN BAKING CORN BREAD, BAKE A SMALL AMOUNT AT A TIME SO YOU WILL BE ABLE TO SERVE THE CORN BREAD HOT.

HOT CORN MUFFINS: Serve 3 corn muffins on a tea plate underlined with a paper doily for A La Carte. Serve 2 muffins for Table d'hôte. Pat of butter on B&B plate.

PREPARATION: Same as Hot Corn Bread, except bake in a greased muffin pan.

HOT CORN STICKS: Serve 4 hot corn sticks on a tea plate underlined with a doily. Pat of butter on a B&B plate for A La Carte.

PREPARATION: Same as Hot Corn Bread, except bake in hot, greased, corn stick pans.

HUSH PUPPIES:

2-cups cornmeal	1 finely chopped onion
1-cup flour	1
teaspoon salt	
2 eggs	milk
3 teaspoons baking powder	

Mix all the dry ingredients and the onion, drop in the eggs, then add enough milk to make a medium batter and stir well. Drop the mixture into hot deep fat a spoonful at a time. Remove when outside is crisp and golden.

MILK TOAST: Serve 3 slices of dry toast cut in quarters in a soup plate. Soup plate underlined with breakfast plate, and a soup tureen of boiling milk with soup ladle in same. Serve pat of butter on B&B plate.

PREPARATION: Same as for dry toast.

RY-KRISP: Serve 4 Ry-Krisp on a tea plate, underlined with a doily.

SALLY LUNN MUFFINS: [Makes about 24, depending on size of the rings.]

4 cups flour   4 eggs
4 teaspoons baking powder
Enough milk to make a batter
1-teaspoon salt
4 kitchenspoons melted butter*
1 kitchenspoon sugar*

PREPARATION: Mix flour, baking powder, salt, and sugar together. Add eggs and sufficient milk to make a batter. Add melted butter. Be careful not to beat batter after butter is added. Merely stir it in. Use only melted butter; no lard or other substitute. Serve 3 muffins on tea plate underlined with a doily. NOTE: WHEN BAKING SALLY LUNN MUFFINS BAKE A SMALL AMOUNT AT A TIME SO THAT YOU WILL BE ABLE TO SERVE THE MUFFINS HOT. Table d'hôte serve 2 muffins.

* 1 kitchenspoon = 4 tablespoons

SOUTHERN CORN CAKES, SYRUP OR HONEY: Serve 4 corn cakes on hot tea plate with cake cover. Syrup or honey on side in syrup jug. Double portion of butter served on B&B plate. A La Carte.

PREPARATION:

2 eggs
2 tablespoons sugar
1 teaspoon salt
2 cups corn meal—white
½ cup white flour
2 teaspoons baking powder

Thin to a batter with milk. Keep fairly thin.

SOUTHERN CORN CAKES, SYRUP OR HONEY, WITH BACON: Prepare and serve 4 cakes with syrup or honey, as shown above. Serve 3 strips of bacon on a hot breakfast plate.

SOUTHERN CORN CAKES, SYRUP OR HONEY, WITH SAUSAGE PATTIES:
Prepare and serve 4 cakes with syrup or honey as shown above. Serve 2 sausage patties on a hot breakfast plate.

ON CLUB BREAKFAST: Same as Breakfast A La Carte, except serve 3 cakes instead of 4.

SOUTHERN WHEAT CAKES WITH SYRUP OR HONEY: Serve 4 wheat cakes on a hot tea plate with cake cover. Syrup or honey on side in syrup jug. Double portion of butter served on B&B plate.

PREPARATION:

2 eggs
2 tablespoons sugar
1 teaspoon salt
2 teaspoons baking powder
2½ cups white flour

>Thin to a batter with milk. Keep fairly thin.

SOUTHERN WHEAT CAKES, SYRUP OR HONEY, WITH BACON: Prepare and serve 4 cakes with syrup or honey, as shown above. Serve 3 strips of bacon on a hot breakfast plate.

SOUTHERN WHEAT CAKES, SYRUP OR HONEY, WITH SAUSAGE PATTIES:
Prepare and serve 4 cakes with syrup or honey as shown above. Serve 2 sausage patties on a hot breakfast plate.

ON CLUB BREAKFAST: Same as Breakfast A La Carte, except serve 3 cakes instead of 4.

WHOLE WHEAT BISCUITS: Serve 3 biscuits on A La Carte and 2 biscuits on Table d'hôte on a tea plate underlined with doily.

2 cups white flour

2 cups whole-wheat flour
4½ teaspoons baking powder
2/3-cup shortening
1½ teaspoons salt
1½ cups milk

PREPARATION: Sift the white flour, measure, and resift 3 times with baking powder and salt. Stir in the unsifted whole-wheat flour. Cut in the shortening. Add milk all at once and stir vigorously with a fork until dough just stiffens up; then turn onto a lightly floured board and knead 8 to 10 times. Roll or pat out to thickness of about 3/8 or ½ inch, and cut out with floured biscuit cutter. Place on greased baking sheet or pan and bake in a hot oven for about 12 minutes. Makes twenty-four [24], 2-inch biscuits.

HOT BISCUITS:

6 coffee cups plain flour
½ teaspoon baking soda
1-teaspoon salt
1½ cups shortening
1-pint buttermilk mixed with ½ pint water
6 teaspoons baking powder

PREPARATION: Sift flour once. Mix thoroughly all dry ingredients. Sift again into mixing pan. Cut in shortening lightly. Add liquid and mix thoroughly with a spoon [this will be a rather wet dough]. Flour breadboard liberally [about ½ to 2/3 cup]. Place about 1/3 of mixture on board and knead about 4 times, flipping dough over each time. Roll out to medium thickness. Cut into biscuits with biscuit cutter. Place in greased baking pan and bake in moderately hot oven until brown. Brush lightly with butter. Care should be taken to avoid unnecessary handling.

SERVICE: Serve 3 biscuits on a tea plate underlined with doily, A La Carte; serve 2 biscuits on Table d'hôte.

HOT ROLLS: We will use half-baked rolls for this service. These rolls should be browned in the oven and served hot. Brown only a few rolls at a time. Serve 3 rolls, 2 white and 1 whole wheat, on a tea plate underlined with doily for A La Carte service. Serve 2 rolls, 1 white and 1 whole wheat for Table d'hôte service.

FRENCH TOAST WITH SYRUP OR HONEY: Beat together one egg, ½ pint of milk, one tablespoon sugar, and two drops of vanilla, making enough mixture for four [4] orders of French Toast.

Trim three slices of toast bread, cut diagonally, dip in mixture coating both sides of bread thoroughly, then fry in hot oil until golden brown. Be sure oil is hot before putting toast in pan to keep toast from being soggy. Sprinkle lightly with sugar on one side. Never use milk in excess of the above ratio, so that mixture retains lemon yellow color.

Serve six diagonal slices of French Toast overlapping on breakfast plate with two individual honey or one individual syrup on bread and butter plate.

This recipe was updated in 1972, while most of the others in this section are from the 1950's. Notice that in an attempt to control costs, the syrup pitcher has been replaced with individual packages of syrup and honey. By the time the Southern Crescent ended service in 1979, the Southern Railway was losing approximately $15,000,000 per year on that one train.

CEREALS

COOKED CEREALS: Serve in oatmeal bowl filling up to the line, underlined with a tea plate and doily. Pitcher of cream on side.

DRY CEREALS: Serve individual package of dry cereal, which has been cut partly through, underlined with a doily and tea plate. Oatmeal bowl underlined with tea plate and doily for service. Pitcher of cream or milk on side.

DESSERTS

BLEU CHEESE WITH CRACKERS: Serve one ¾ ounce portion of Bleu Cheese, partly unwrapped on a tea plate underlined with doily, with two individual packages of Waverly Wafers or one individual package of Strietmann Club Crackers on same plate. This service to be the same on Table d'hôte and A La Carte as the price of A La Carte Bleu Cheese has been reduced to 45¢.

BREAD AND BUTTER PUDDING, VANILLA SAUCE: Grease sides and bottom of pudding pan, then dice bread placing layer on bottom of pan, sprinkle with sugar and butter and a little cinnamon between each layer of bread until pan is full. Beat 2 eggs, with 3 cups of milk with a little salt. Pour this over bread, let stand one hour then bake slowly for ¾ hour, then uncover and brown. Serve in fruit saucer underlined with doily and tea plate. Spoonful of vanilla sauce on top. A La Carte, serve in oatmeal bowl.

VANILLA SAUCE: Use prepared vanilla pudding mixture, cutting the pudding to the proper consistency for a sauce.

BREAKFAST FIGS: Use canned figs. Serve 4 or 5 figs, depending on size, with some of the juice in an oatmeal bowl underlined with doily and tea plate, with pitcher of cream on side.

CHOCOLATE CAKE:

Cream together [in order]:

1 Cup Butter
2 Cups Sugar
2 Eggs
Pinch Salt
2 Teaspoons Vanilla
1 Cup Sour Milk [add 1 teaspoon white vinegar to milk]
3 Cups Flour
2 Teaspoons Baking Soda in 1 Cup Warm Water
2/3 Cup Cocoa

Bake at 350 1 hour in 1 pan, or 30-35 minutes in 2 pans.

CHOCOLATE SUNDAE: Table d'hôte: Serve one level No. 12 scoop of ice cream in fruit saucer, or one slice of brick ice cream, well covered with chocolate sauce. For A La Carte service serve one heaping No. 12 scoop of ice cream in fruit saucer [do not level the scoop as for Table d'hôte], or two slices of brick ice cream in oatmeal bowl well covered with chocolate sauce. Underline with tea plate and doily. Ice cream spoon on right side for service.

CHOCOLATE SAUCE: Order from Commissary.

DEEP DISH APPLE PIE: Use frozen apples which have been sweetened or unsweetened canned apples that should be sweetened, placing a liberal portion in individual deep pie dish. Season with butter and nutmeg. Cover with top crust. Cut 2 or 3 holes in top crust to let steam escape. Brush with milk and bake until done and brown. No bottom crust. Serve individual pie on tea plate underlined with doily.

PIE CRUST RECIPE:

3 cups sifted flour
1-cup lard
1 teaspoon salt
2/3 cup ice water
2 teaspoons butter

Work shortening into flour with finger tips. Add cold water a little at a time. Cut and chop dough with fork. Handle as little as possible. The least water used the better. Place on lightly floured board, roll and shape as desired.

DEEP DISH BERRY PIE: Use frozen or fresh berries which should be sweetened with sugar, placing a liberal portion in individual deep pie dish with dash of nutmeg over berries. Cover with top crust only. Cut 2 or 3 holes in top crust to let steam escape. Brush with milk and bake until done and brown. No bottom crust. Serve individual pie on tea plate underlined with doily. A La Mode: Serve same as above except serve slice of ice cream or ice cream scoop of ice cream on top of pie.

PIE CRUST RECIPE: Same as Deep Dish Apple Pie

BREAD AND BUTTER, RAISIN, PUDDING—VANILLA SAUCE: Grease sides and bottom of pudding pan, then dice bread placing layer on bottom of pan, sprinkle with sugar, raisins, and butter and a little cinnamon between each layer of bread until pan is full. Beat 2 eggs, with 3 cups of milk with a little salt. Pour this over bread, let stand one hour. Cover and bake slowly for ¾ hour, then uncover and brown. Serve in fruit saucer underlined with doily and tea plate. Spoonful of vanilla sauce on top. A La Carte, serve in oatmeal bowl.

VANILLA SAUCE: Use prepared vanilla pudding mixture, cutting the pudding to the proper consistency for a sauce.

STRAWBERRY CHEESE CAKE: 10 orders out of a cheese cake, top with fresh sweetened strawberries or frozen strawberries. Serve on a chilled tea plate.
Cheese cake should be thawed in refrigerator for 8 to 10 hours.

Note—For SCRM Service, all pies will be prepared in advance and notes for service adapted accordingly.

DEEP DISH CHERRY PIE:

1 #10 can of cherries, or 6 #2 cans
4 cups sugar
¾ tablespoon corn starch, dissolved in ¼ cup water

PREPARATION: Empty cherries into colander and drain well. Add sugar to juice, bring to boil, then cook until juice is reduced to half. Add cherries and cook 10 minutes. Add corn starch. Stir well and boil 5 minutes more. Remove from fire; pour into crock and cool. Place cooled cherries in 5 oz. Deep dish and cover with top crust in which holes have been cut to allow steam to escape. Brush with milk and bake until done and brown. No bottom crust. Serve individual pie on tea plate underlined with doily.

PIE CRUST RECIPE: Same as Deep Dish Apple Pie.

DEEP DISH PEACH PIE: Use frozen peaches which have already been sweetened or canned peaches which should be sweetened with sugar, placing a liberal portion in individual deep pie dish with dash of nutmeg over peaches. Cover with top crust only. Cut 2 or 3 holes in top crust to let steam escape. Brush with milk and bake until done and brown. No bottom crust. Serve individual pie on tea plate underlined with doily.

PIE CRUST RECIPE: Same as Deep Dish Apple Pie.

HOT MINCE PIE, CHEESE: [Pastry for 4 pies—top and bottom crusts.]

6 cups flour
½ cup butter
1 tablespoon salt
1 cup shortening
1½ cups of ice water

PREPARATION: Sift flour and salt together in a mixing bowl, cut in shortening and work until well mixed and of coarse grain. Add ice water and mix well together. Pat dough together into solid lump, covering with damp towel, place on platter and set in chill box. Line tins with paste [dough] and fill with mince meat which should be used just as it comes from can. Nothing should be added. Moisten edges of bottom crust with little water and cover with top crust in which 2 or 3 holes have been made to allow steam to escape. Brush top crust with milk, then bake until brown and done [about 45-50 minutes]. Serve 1/6 cut of pie and pat of American Cheese on tea plate for Table d'hôte. Serve 1/5 cut of pie and pat of American Cheese on tea plate for A La Carte service.

ICE CREAM: Table d'hôte: Serve one level No. 12 scoop of ice cream in fruit saucer or one slice of brick ice cream. If brick, ice cream must be unwrapped in pantry. For A La Carte service serve one heaping No. 12 scoop of ice cream in fruit saucer [do not level the scoop as for Table d'hôte] or two slices of brick ice cream in oatmeal bowl. Underline with doily and tea plate. Teaspoon on right hand side for service.

ICE CREAM WAFERS: Serve one level No. 12 scoop of ice cream in fruit saucer or one slice of brick ice cream. If brick, ice cream must be unwrapped in pantry. Serve in fruit saucer underlined with doily and tea plate. 3 wafers on left hand side of tea plate and teaspoon on right hand side for service.

PINEAPPLE SUNDAE: Table d'hôte: Serve one level No. 12 scoop of ice cream in fruit saucer or one slice of brick ice cream, well covered with crushed pineapple. For A La Carte service serve one heaping No. 12 scoop of ice cream in fruit saucer [do not level the scoop as for Table d'hôte] or two slices of brick ice cream in oatmeal bowl well covered with crushed pineapple. Underline with tea plate and doily. Ice cream spoon on right hand side for service.

PEACH COBBLER:

½ cup self rising flour   ½ cup milk
½ cup sugar   ½ cup butter

Mix the above ingredients into a batter. Dot bottom of baking dish with butter. Pour the batter into the dish. Add 2 cups peaches, sweetened slightly. Bake 30-45 minutes, until top is lightly browned.

PEACH SHORTCAKE, WHIPPED CREAM: Use shortcake sheets cut into 3" squares. Split in half, placing spoonful of sliced frozen peaches on bottom half of square, then place top half sheet on top of this with another spoonful of sliced peaches on top. Cover with whipped cream and top with a slice of peach. Serve on tea plate.

RICE-RAISIN PUDDING, VANILLA SAUCE: Place washed rice into boiling water and cook 10 minutes. Drain and rinse. Set blanched rice to boil in the milk. Add sugar and cook until soft. Beat eggs, vanilla, and salt with the half-cup cream and soak seedless raisins. Add to the boiled rice. Mix well. Cook in baking pan. Serve with spoonful of vanilla sauce poured over same in fruit saucer underlined with doily and tea plate on Table d'hôte. On A La Carte serve in oatmeal bowl.

What's fascinating about this recipe is the only measurement given is for a half cup of cream, yet the cooks knew enough to be able to turn out what appears to be a tasty dessert.

VANILLA SAUCE: Use prepared vanilla pudding mixture and reduce to the proper consistency for a sauce.

SOUR CREAM COFFEE CAKE:

Cream ¼ pound butter with 1 cup sugar. Add 2 unbeaten eggs, ½ pint sour cream, and 1 teaspoon vanilla. Beat well.

Sift 1 teaspoon baking powder, 1 teaspoon baking soda, and 2 cups flour. Add to batter and beat well.

Sugar mixture: Mix together ½ cup chopped walnuts, ¼ cup sugar, and 1 teaspoon cinnamon.

Grease pan with hole in the middle. Put 1/3 of sugar mixture in pan, then ½ of the batter. Then 1/3 of the sugar mixture and the rest of the batter, and top with remaining sugar mixture. Bake 40-45 minutes in 350 degree oven.

STRAWBERRY SHORTCAKE, WHIPPED CREAM: Use shortcake sheets cut into 3" squares. Split in half, placing spoonful of strawberries on bottom half of square, then place top half sheet on top of this with another spoonful of strawberries on top. Cover with whipped cream and top with a whole strawberry. Serve on tea plate.

STRAWBERRY SUNDAE: Table d'hôte: Serve one level No. 12 scoop of ice cream in fruit saucer, or one slice of brick ice cream. Pour dessert spoonful of strawberry topping over ice cream. For A La Carte service serve one heaping No. 12 scoop of ice cream in fruit saucer [do not level the scoop as for Table d'hôte] or two slices of brick ice cream in oatmeal bowl with dessert spoonful of strawberry topping poured over ice cream. Underline with tea plate and doily. Ice cream spoon on right side for service.

STRAWBERRY TOPPING: Order from Commissary.

SWEET POTATO PIE: [Ingredients for 3 pies]

1 quart sweet potatoes, mashed
3 teaspoons nutmeg
4 eggs well whipped
Juice of ½ lemon
3½ cups sugar
½ pint cream
¼ cup melted butter

Cut ends of potatoes off to keep them from being stringy and boil in jackets until well done. Mash well and add butter, eggs, sugar, nutmeg, lemon juice, and cream. Mix well. Place mixture in pie shell and cook in moderate oven until done. Serve 1/6 cut of pie on tea plate for Table d'hôte service. Serve 1/5 cut of pie on tea plate for A La Carte service.

PIE CRUST RECIPE: Same as Deep Dish Apple Pie.

APPLE PIE, CHEESE: [Pastry for 4 pies—top and bottom crusts.]

6 cups flour
½ cup butter
1 tablespoon salt
1 cup shortening
1½ cups ice water

PREPARATION: Sift flour and salt together in mixing bowl, cut in shortening and work until well mixed and of coarse grain. Add ice water and mix well together. Pat dough into solid lump, covering with damp towel, place on platter and set in chill box. Line tins with paste [dough]. For each pie, take 2/3-cup sugar and 1 tablespoon flour and mix. Sprinkle about ¼ of this mixture on bottom of unbaked shell. Fill shell with canned apples and sprinkle the remaining sugar and flour mixture on top of apples. Season with butter, lemon juice, and nutmeg. Moisten edges of bottom crust with a little water and cover with top crust in which 2 or 3 holes have been made to allow steam to escape. Brush top crust with milk, then bake until brown and done [about 45-50 minutes]. Serve 1/6 cut of pie and pat of American Cheese on tea plate for Table d'hôte Service. Serve 1/5 cut of pie and pat of American Cheese on tea plate for A La Carte service.

OLD FASHIONED STRAWBERRY SHORTCAKE, WHIPPED CREAM:

4 cups flour
1-teaspoon salt
2 tablespoons baking powder
2/3-cup shortening
1 tablespoon melted butter
1½ cups milk
2 tablespoons sugar

Sift flour. Measure and resift with baking powder and salt three times. Cut in shortening until particles are size of rice grains. Add milk all at once and mix lightly and quickly with a fork. With lightly floured hand, pat out on lightly floured board to uniform thickness and cut with 3½-inch biscuit cutter. Brush with butter and sprinkle with sugar. Place on well-greased baking pan and bake in hot oven for 15 to 18 minutes until rich crusty brown. Slice while warm, butter cut surface and serve with liberal portion of strawberries between biscuit on tea plate covered well with whipped cream and topped with a whole or half strawberry.

APPLE BROWN BETTY, LEMON SAUCE: In a greased round baking pan place a layer of bread crumbs using half whole wheat and half white bread crumbs, then a layer of chopped stewed apples. Sprinkle this with nutmeg, lemon juice, and cinnamon, bits of butter and a little sugar. Then continue placing a layer of bread crumbs and apples and seasoning until the pan is filled, ending with bread crumbs. Set aside a few minutes until the top layer of bread crumbs is absorbed, then place in a moderate oven and bake until done. Serve in fruit saucer underlined with doily and tea plate, with lemon sauce poured over pudding for Table d'hôte service. On A La Carte service, serve in oatmeal bowl. Note: We will use #10 canned apples for this service.

LEMON SAUCE: Use prepared lemon pudding mixture, cutting the pudding to the proper consistency for a sauce.

PECAN PIE: [Ingredients for 4 pies—bottom crust only]

2¼ cups sugar
10 eggs
2 cups fine toasted bread crumbs [½ white toast and ½ whole wheat toast]
8 cups syrup [dark Karo]
½ tablespoon salt
½ tablespoon vanilla
1 cup butter
3 cups pecans

Place bread in oven and dry out thoroughly and then roll fine with rolling pin. Cream together well sugar, bread crumbs, salt, and butter. Add eggs slowly. Then add syrup and last add vanilla. Pour in unbaked pie shell and sprinkle pecans evenly over the pies before placing in oven. Bake in medium oven for approximately 30 minutes or until done. Serve 1/6 cut of pie on tea plate for Table d'hôte service. Serve 1/5 cut of pie on tea plate for A La Carte service.

KENTUCKY BOURBON CHOCOLATE PECAN PIE: [bottom crust only]

1 Cup sugar
1 Cup light corn syrup
½ Cup better or margarine
4 Eggs, lightly beaten
¼ Cup Bourbon
1 Teaspoon vanilla extract
¼ Teaspoon salt

1 cup semisweet chocolate chips
1 cup pecan pieces
1 Unbaked 9-inch deep dish pie crust

Preheat oven to 325° F. Combine first 3 ingredients in a small saucepan and cook over medium heat, stirring constantly, until butter melts and sugar dissolves. Stir in chocolate chips. Cool slightly. Beat eggs, bourbon, vanilla, and salt in a large bowl, gradually add sugar mixture, beating well with a wire whisk, add pecans, pour into pastry shell. Bake for 50 to 55 minutes, or until set. Serve warm or chilled.

PIE CRUST RECIPE: [Bottom crust only]

3 cups flour
¼ cup butter
¾ cup ice water
1 teaspoon salt
½ cup shortening

PREPARATION: Sift flour and salt together in a mixing bowl, cut in shortening and work until well mixed and of coarse grain. Add ice water and mix well together. Pat dough together into solid lump, covering with damp towel, place on platter and set in chill box. Line tins with paste [dough].

YULE LOG:

This item was only served during the holiday season and was ordered, pre-made, from the commissary.

6 eggs, separated
2 heaping tablespoons cocoa
1 heaping tablespoon self rising flour
1 teaspoon baking powder
1 cup sugar

Whip whites, not dry. Beat egg yolks, add sugar to the yolks. Sift the dry ingredients and add to the yolks. Fold into the whites. Bake in a jelly roll pan at 350 degrees about a half hour or until springy. [I use parchment paper in the pan because it helps with the next step]. Turn out onto a damp towel and roll it like you would a jelly roll.

When it's cooled:

1 pint heavy cream
1 tablespoon sugar
1 teaspoon vanilla

Add the sugar and vanilla to the cream. Whip until real stiff. Unroll the cake and spread the cream over it. Roll it back up.

You probably noticed that many of these recipes called for either canned or frozen fruit. Although fresh fruit was used whenever possible, and gave variety depending on what was available at certain times of the year, canned and frozen fruits offered the advantage of consistent quality and consistent prices.

When Train Tickets Were Money

In the mid 1870's, South Carolina was in an economic depression. The state was still suffering from the effects of the Civil War and reconstruction. Money was hard to come by. As a way to raise some much needed capital, the South Carolina Rail Road [a Southern Railway predecessor] issued what they called "fare tickets". These tickets were issued in whole amounts of one, two, five, ten, and twenty dollars. The One Dollar fare ticket allowed a single passenger to be transported 25 miles, for a rate of 4 cents per mile. The other tickets had similar values.

In effect, the railroad printed its own money. These "fare tickets" were promises to transport, and the "News and Courier" newspaper in Charleston was accepting these tickets as payment for subscriptions or for advertising. The difference between the "fare tickets" and regular money is that they were not backed by gold or silver in government vaults, or by deposits in local banks. Rather, they were backed by the promise of the railroad to provide an equivalent dollar value in transportation at some future time.

Money, in and of itself, whether paper or coins, has little value. It can't be eaten, you can't wear it; it cannot shelter you. Its value comes from the potential goods and services it represents— what you can buy with it. Money serves as a medium of exchange; it provides a means to allow people to obtain that which they could not acquire through bartering. But, in the final analysis, money must be backed by goods and services, or it will have no value. It is in that very basic sense that the "fare tickets" were money.

EGGS

Boiled, fried, or scrambled, as desired by guest. If boiled, serve in egg glass underlined with doily and tea plate. If fried or scrambled, serve on breakfast plate, garnished with parsley.

SAUSAGE, BACON, AND STREAK-O-LEAN BACON: All cars are being furnished with a bacon broiler and all sausage, bacon, and streak-o-lean bacon should be cooked in the oven in this bacon broiler as there will be less shrinkage and these items can be better prepared in this way. Sausage, bacon, and streak-o-lean bacon must be placed on paper towels to absorb excess grease.

> WHEN COOKING THIS BACON OR SAUSAGE IN THE OVEN, COOKS SHOULD BE CAREFUL NOT TO LET A SURPLUS OF GREASE ACCUMULATE IN THIS BACON BROILER AS IT MUST BE POURED OFF. CHEFS WILL SEE THAT BACON, SAUSAGE, AND STREAK-O-LEAN BACON IS NOT PREPARED ON TOP OF THE RANGE, BUT IN THIS BACON BROILER ONLY. PROPER CARE MUST BE TAKEN OF THESE BACON BROILERS AND NOT ALLOWED TO BECOME CAKED WITH BURNT GREASE, ETC.

Streak-o-lean bacon is getting hard to find. It's basically fatback, with a strip of lean meat running through it.

BACON WITH EGGS: Serve two eggs, three strips of bacon on breakfast plate. Garnish with parsley.

BROILED SUGAR-CURED HAM WITH EGGS: Serve ½ slice of ham with two eggs on breakfast plate. Garnish with parsley. **Note:** Ham is not to be horseshoed, but a whole slice of ham to be cut across, and through bone, and slice ham in half.

KIPPERED HERRING WITH SCRAMBLED EGGS: Scramble eggs as usual. Kippered herring will be furnished in individual 3¼ oz. tins. Empty the contents of one tin into frying pan with a little butter. Do not fry brown, but heat thoroughly, being careful not to break up the fish. Serve on breakfast plate with eggs. Garnish with parsley.

OUR OWN SPECIAL COUNTRY SAUSAGE WITH TWO EGGS: Serve two cakes of sausage with two eggs as desired by guest on breakfast plate. Garnish with parsley.

PAN BROWNED CORNED BEEF HASH WITHPOACHED EGG: Take a liberal amount of browned corned beef hash, which should be browned in frying pan. Form in oblong shape. Serve on breakfast plate with poached egg resting on top. Garnish with parsley.

POACHED EGG ON TOAST: Serve two poached eggs resting on toast on breakfast plate. Garnish with parsley.

THIS SERVICE FOR TRAINS 47-48 AND 38-37 ONLY

SPECIAL BREAKFAST $2.00 OLD FASHIONED COUNTRY CURED HAM, NATURAL GRAVY, WITH EGGS: Serve slice of ham, resting in red gravy, with two eggs on breakfast plate. Garnish with parsley. IN THE SERVICE OF THIS HAM A SERRATED BLADE KNIFE [STEAK KNIFE] MUST BE SERVED. Ham is not to be horseshoed, but whole slice of ham to be cut, saw through bone. Cut this ham in portions similar size to the sugar-cured ham you are now serving. Some of these hams are quite large and when you get to the large center slices of this ham, the chef should be able to get more than two portions to the slice. WHEN GRITS ARE REQUESTED WITH THIS ORDER, YOU WILL SERVE GRITS IN FRUIT SAUCER ON SIDE. THIS HAM IS NOT TO BE CONSUMED BY MEMBERS OF THE DINING CAR CREWS. The surplus fat from these hams should be used for seasoning of vegetables. The hocks and ends of these hams should be used for minced ham and eggs and also chopped ham omelet. Reorder ham as needed.

FOWL

<u>BONELESS CHICKEN FRICASSEE, RICE:</u> Boiled fowl, boned and separated into pieces. Ingredients for ½ gallon of sauce:

½ cup chicken fat or butter
1 cup flour
1½ quarts chicken broth
½ cup cream and 2 egg yolks, beaten together

<u>PREPARATION:</u> Make a roux from fat and flour. Let cook about 10 minutes. Add boiling chicken broth slowly, beating constantly with egg whip to prevent lumps. Season with salt and let cook about 20 minutes. Remove from range; add cream to which beaten egg yolks have been added. Let come to boiling point only. Strain and use. Serve liberal portion of white and dark meat on toast, on medium platter, with sauce. AD cup of rice on side of chicken. Garnish with parsley. Breakfast plate for service. Table d'hôte: serve on breakfast plate, garnish with parsley.

<u>BROILED YOUNG CHICKEN, BACON:</u> Wash and clean chicken well. Serve ½ chicken broiled properly. Serve on hot medium platter, breakfast plate for service. Garnish with 1/8 lemon and sprig of parsley. Frill on leg bone. 2 strips of broiled bacon over chicken. Table d'hôte: serve on hot dinner plate.

<u>CHICKEN SHORTCAKE, SOUTHERN STYLE:</u> Boiled fowl, skinned, boned, and separated into pieces. Serve on medium platter, breakfast plate for service. Garnish with parsley. Table d'hôte: serve on breakfast plate. Garnish with sprig of parsley.

Ingredients for 1 gallon of sauce

1 cup chicken fat or butter
2 cups flour
3 quarts chicken broth
1-8 oz. can mushrooms

1 cup cream and 4 egg yolks, beaten together

PREPARATION: Make a roux from fat and flour. Let cook about 10 minutes. Add boiling chicken broth slowly, beating constantly with egg whip to prevent lumps. Season with salt and let cook about 20 minutes. Remove from range; add cream to which beaten egg yolks have been added. Let come to boiling point only. Strain, add mushrooms and use.

Prepare cornbread in baking pan about ¾ inch thick. Cut corn bread into pieces 2½ inches by 4 inches. Split cornbread and place a layer of chicken on the bottom piece, then cover with the top piece, and place some chicken on top of it. Then cover with liberal portion of sauce.

CHICKEN AND HAM SHORTCAKE, SOUTHERN: Same as Chicken Shortcake, Southern Style, except add an equal amount of chopped ham to boiled fowl, skinned, boned, and separated into pieces.

CHICKEN AND RICE CASSEROLE:

1 cup uncooked rice	1 teaspoon onion salt
1 teaspoon parsley flakes	1 can cream of
mushroom soup	
1 teaspoon celery salt	¾ cup water

Stir together and put into a long greased pan. Cut up chicken and sprinkle with salt Spread with mayonnaise. Lay on rice with skin side up. Cover pan with foil and bake 2 hours at 300 degrees. If not browned enough, place under broiler.

FRIED CHICKEN SOUTHERN STYLE, CREAM GRAVY: Singe, wash and split in half. Then unjoint. Do not chop. Season with salt and pepper. Roll in flour; fry chicken slowly in lard until of golden color. Chicken must be kept covered while frying. Remove and keep hot. To serve, cover bottom of medium platter with gravy and lay the chicken in gravy. Frill on legbone. Garnish with parsley. Breakfast plate for service. Table d'hôte: serve on hot dinner plate.

CREAM GRAVY: Make a cream gravy, adding sufficient flour to the grease that chicken was fried in, stirring until it gets thick. Then add milk, stirring continually to keep from lumping. Season by adding salt.

Here's an updated version of the fried chicken, making it healthier. Use skinless chicken breasts. Wash, season with salt [or substitute] and pepper, then roll in flour. Fry chicken slowly in Olive Oil, until done. Drain most of the oil from frying pan. Make the gravy as above, substituting 2% milk for whole milk. Serve as above.

INDIVIDUAL CHICKEN PIE, EN CASSEROLE: Serve in casserole, underlined with doily and tea plate, breakfast plate for service. One boiled chicken makes 4 or 5 pies, using breast, first, and second joints.

Ingredients for ½ gallon of sauce:

1 cup butter
1 cup flour
1 pt. Parisian potatoes, cooked in salt water
1½ quarts chicken broth
Green Peas
Fried Bacon

PREPARATION: Make a roux from butter and flour [not too thick]. Let cook about 10 minutes, add boiling chicken broth slowly, beating with egg whip to prevent lumps. Season with salt, let cook not less than 20 minutes, strain and use as follows:

Place 3 pieces dark, 2 white meat, ½ strip fried bacon, 6 Parisian potatoes, and 1 tablespoon green peas in casserole, add sufficient sauce, cover with pie dough in which 2 or 3 holes have been cut to allow steam to escape. Bake in hot oven until crust is done and well browned. Use Parisian cutter for making potato balls.

PIE CRUST RECIPE: Same as Deep Dish Apple Pie.

INDIVIDUAL CHICKEN PIE, SOUTHERN: Same as Individual Chicken Pie, En Casserole.

ROAST YOUNG TURKEY, DRESSING, CRANBERRY SAUCE: Serve equal portions light and dark meat on bed of dressing on medium platter, cranberry sauce in #45 ramekin on same platter. Garnish with parsley. Breakfast plate for service. Turkey must be neatly sliced [turkey to be sliced to order]. Table d'hôte: serve on breakfast plate.

PREPARATION: Singe, draw [be sure to remove lungs], wash well and dry. Tie turkey; season with salt and pepper. Place in roasting pan, and add 2 onions and 2 stalks of celery. Pour a little fat over turkey and roast, frequently turning over when necessary so it will brown evenly. After 15 minutes of roasting it will probably be necessary to add a little stock to the pan to prevent burning of vegetables.

GIBLET GRAVY: Rinse both gizzards and livers well in cold water. Put the necks and gizzards into sauce pan, add water and salt. Cover and cook until very tender. The last half-hour add the livers and hearts and cook until tender. Pull all the meat off the neck and chop with livers, gizzards, and hearts into small pieces. Remove turkey from pan, pour off surplus fat, place pan on top of range, dust vegetables with ½ cup flour, make a roux and brown well. Add 1 cup of stewed tomatoes and 1½ quarts of chicken stock. Let come to boil and cook for at least 30 minutes. Add the chopped gizzards, livers, hearts, and meat off the neck the last 15 minutes of cooking.

CRANBERRY SAUCE: Use canned cranberry sauce.

DRESSING:

2 cups of minced onions
2 teaspoons poultry seasoning
2 cups of minced celery

Sauté the above ingredients in poultry fat. Take about 4 quarts of bread mixture including leftover bran muffins, corn muffins or corn bread, and toast, which should be broken up into small pieces, and two cakes of cooked sausage that has been ground or chopped fine for this mixture. Re-heat, breaking all up together and moisten with poultry stock while warm. Mix well with other ingredients, but do not brown or dry out. Serve hot.

STEWED CHICKEN, CREOLE, EN CASSEROLE: Use stewed chicken, cut into pieces about 2 inches long, dark and white. Place chicken in sauce pan with Creole sauce. Simmer five or ten minutes. Serve in casserole underlined with tea plate and doily with an AD cup of rice on top. Breakfast plate for service.

CREOLE SAUCE:

1 clove
6 medium onions
6 green peppers
1 #1 can pimentoes, 1" slices
1 button garlic
2 #3 cans tomatoes
1 #1 can French or small peas
1 #1 can mushrooms, sliced

PREPARATION: Sauté onions, peppers [sliced in 1 inch Julienne] and garlic about 5 minutes. Add tomatoes, mushrooms, simmer about 30 minutes. Finish with peas and pimentoes.

BROILED CHICKEN, SMITHFIELD: Wash and clean chicken well. Serve ½ chicken broiled properly. Serve on hot dinner plate. Garnish with 1/8 lemon and sprig of parsley. Frill on leg bone. Small piece of broiled Smithfield ham on top of chicken.

CHICKEN CROQUETTES, SAUCE SUPREME: [ingredients for 9 portions]
Two croquettes to portion, cooked to order.
1 chicken, cooked, skinned, boned, cut into ¼" dice
½ cup chicken fat
1 cup flour
2 cups chicken broth

2 egg yolks

PREPARATION: Melt fat, add flour and make a roux. Then add boiling chicken broth and cook until sauce is thick and pasty. Add chicken meat, mix well, and let slowly cook about 10 minutes. Stir in egg yolks. Season with salt and pepper. Turn mixture into a shallow pan, smooth with pallet knife and cover with greased paper. When mixture is cold, form into cone shapes. Bread with Redi-Breader and fry in deep fat. When brown, remove and place on clean paper towel to absorb fat. On A La Carte serve three croquettes on medium platter, breakfast plate for service. On Table d'hôte serve two croquettes on breakfast plate. Garnish with parsley.

SAUCE: [Ingredients for ½ gallon]

1 cup flour
½ cup butter
Salt
1½ quarts boiling milk

PREPARATION: Melt butter in sauce pan. Add flour and make a roux. Let cook at least 10 minutes, to which add boiling milk gradually, stirring constantly with egg whip to prevent sauce's getting lumpy. Cook 30 minutes. Season with salt only. Strain into crock and place small bits of butter on top to prevent crust from forming.

SOUTHERN BARBECUE CHICKEN:

Grill ½ chicken until done, turning once. About 10 minutes before chicken is done, baste with Southern Barbecue Sauce. Remove chicken from grill when done, unjoint, but do not chop. Dinner plate for service.

The First Railroad in the South

The first railroad in the south was chartered in 1827 in Charleston, South Carolina. The South Carolina Canal and Rail Road Company built what was the longest railroad in the world, running 136 miles from Charleston to Hamburg, SC [near Augusta, Georgia].

The railroad began the first scheduled passenger train operations on Christmas Day, 1830. The locomotive, The Best Friend of Charleston, was the first American designed, American built steam locomotive to be run on a railroad. A contemporary report of that first trip describes the 15 mph speed as "annihilating space and time and leaving all the world behind".

The railroad survived a major flood in the 1840's, the Civil War, a devastating earthquake, and several bankruptcies and was eventually purchased by the Southern Railway in 1899.

Among the railroad's other firsts:

- The first night operations
- The first scheduled passenger trains
- One of the first to have sleeping cars
- The first railroad junction [at Branchville, SC]
- One of the first to carry the U. S. Mail

FRUITS

<u>BAKED APPLE WITH CREAM:</u> Serve in cereal bowl, underlined with doily and tea plate. Pitcher of cream on side.

<u>PREPARATION:</u> Use size 72 apples. Core apples carefully, then peel down half of the apple, then score with fork. Set into baking pan, add peelings and cores. Put a thin slice of lemon on top of each apple. Sprinkle with sugar, being careful that core holes are filled with sugar. Add ½ cup water. Place in medium oven and bake. Cooks will see that apples are basted while cooking and cook until apples are soft, but must not over-bake apples. Remove from pan and let cool slightly and baste until syrup will adhere to apples. Remove to clean pan. To pan in which they were baked, add ½ cup of water to make a syrup. Let boil 10 minutes and strain. After apples are baked, remove lemon. Serve apples and two spoonfuls syrup poured over.

<u>CHILLED MELON:</u> Serve on tea plate underlined with doily. Cantaloupe: Serve ½ of 46 size melon. Honeydew or Persian: Serve a liberal slice on tea plate underlined with doily, 1/8 lemon served on side of plate with Honeydew melon only. Watermelon [when served on Luncheon and Dinner menu]: Serve a slice of long melon or 1/2 slice of round melon about two inches thick, with rind removed. Serve on chilled dinner plate.

<u>FIGS WITH CREAM:</u> Use canned figs. Serve 4 or 5 whole figs, depending on size, with some of the juice, in oatmeal bowl underlined with doily and tea plate, with pitcher of cream on side.

<u>HALF GRAPEFRUIT:</u> Use size 46 grapefruit only. Roll, cut in half and remove all seeds in each section and loosen grapefruit segments with grapefruit knife. Serve on tea plate, underlined with doily. Finger bowl for service.

<u>STEWED PRUNES WITH CREAM:</u> Serve 1 individual can of prunes in oatmeal bowl underlined with doily and tea plate. Pitcher of cream on side.

SPECIAL FRUIT PLATTER:

CHILLED FLORIDA ORANGE JUICE: Serve in juice glass underlined with fruit saucer.

On a chilled large platter lined with lettuce leaves, place on one end of platter 4 slices of avocado pear. On the other end of the platter place 8 cubes of melon. 3 sections of an orange, ½ pear, 4 sections of grapefruit, ½ peach, 2 stewed prunes, and ½ banana sliced lengthwise. In the center of the platter place 1 slice of pineapple, hole filled with cottage cheese.

TASTY CREAM DRESSING:

PREPARATION: 1 part mayonnaise and 1 part coffee cream mixed together until of creamy consistency. Serve in gravy boat on side.

SERVICE: Serve choice of crackers or Ry-Krisp, or bread and butter on tea plate underlined with doily. An additional chilled tea plate and dessert spoon for service.

CHOICE OF BEVERAGE AND DESSERT: Same as on Table d'hôte meal.

THIS PLATTER SHOULD BE MADE AS ATTRACTIVE AS POSSIBLE.

The following fruits should be fresh: Oranges, Grapefruits, Bananas, Avocado Pears, and Melons.

The following fruits should be canned: Peaches, Pears, Prunes, and Pineapple.

JUICES

GRAPEFRUIT JUICE: Use canned grapefruit juice. Serve in juice glass underlined with fruit saucer.

LEMON JUICE: Serve the juice of 1 lemon in juice glass, underlined with fruit saucer. If water desired, finish filling glass with water.

ORANGE JUICE: Oranges to be quartered and squeezed in orange juicer, to order, not in advance. Orange juice glass for regular portion, water tumbler full for double portion. Underline with fruit saucer. NOTE: Where frozen orange juice concentrate is used, follow directions on can and serve as above.

TOMATO JUICE: Serve in juice glass underlined with fruit saucer, 1/8 lemon in saucer on side of glass.

APPLE JUICE: Serve in juice glass underlined with fruit saucer. Keep juice well chilled.

PINEAPPLE JUICE: Serve in juice glass underlined with fruit saucer. Keep juice well chilled.

MEATS

ASSORTED COLD CUTS, POTATO SALAD: Serve on cold medium platter with AD cup mold of potato salad, a slice of beef, cheese, ham, and tongue, underlined with lettuce leaves. Discretion should be used as to number of pieces of meat to be served according to size of slices. Garnish with slice of dill pickle and slice of tomato and parsley. Table d'hôte: serve on breakfast plate. When menu calls for liverwurst, order liverwurst by the pound, and serve in place of beef.

POTATO SALAD:

3 hard boiled eggs, sliced thin
8 cups cold boiled potatoes, sliced thin
2 tablespoons onions, very finely chopped
1 tablespoon parsley, finely chopped; add a cup of mayonnaise dressing. Season with salt and pepper. Keep very cold.

BAKED SUGAR-CURED HAM, CIDER SAUCE: Tenderized hams do not require boiling. Set ham in baking pan, pour about a cupful of water into pan and bake until nearly done; then skin the ham, and make a seasoning consisting of dry mustard, powdered cloves, and sugar, and place same on ham and put back in oven until glazed. Serve on medium platter with ham resting in cider sauce. Garnish with parsley. Breakfast plate for service. Table d'hôte, serve on breakfast plate.

CIDER SAUCE: [Ingredients for 1 quart]

1½ pt. Beef stock [Ham or chicken stock will do]
1 pt. Apple juice
1 teaspoon salt
¼ teaspoon pepper
¼ cup brown sugar
½ cup butter
½ cup flour

Combine all ingredients except stock. Simmer 10 minutes until chestnut brown. Add hot stock and whip smooth.

BAKED SUGAR-CURED HAM, RAISIN SAUCE: Same as Baked Sugar-Cured Ham, Cider Sauce.

RAISIN SAUCE: To 1 quart of water, add 1 cup of blanched raisins, 1 teaspoon sugar, juice of ½ lemon and let come to boil. Then simmer for 10 minutes.

BREADED PORK CHOPS, TOMATO SAUCE: Chops about ½ inch thick. Season with salt and pepper. Pour some Redi-Breader in shallow pan or dish. Moisten well the pork chops to be breaded and roll them in Redi-Breader, padding well, covering them thoroughly. Repeat operation if heavier coating is desired. Fry in pan, in plenty of fat [if too little is used, breading will burn in spots] until brown. Remove; place in paper towel to remove surplus fat. Place chops in baking pan, sprinkle with a little melted butter, set in hot oven, and leave until well done. Serve on medium platter, resting in sauce. Breakfast plate for service. Table d'hôte: serve on breakfast plate.

TOMATO SAUCE: Use canned tomato soup, which you will use just as it comes out of the can for tomato sauce. Heat and serve.

BREADED VEAL CUTLETS, MILANAISE: Cutlets will come cut 4 to the pound and you will order by the pound as needed. Season with salt and pepper. Pour some Redi-Breader in shallow pan or dish. Moisten well the cutlets to be breaded and roll in Redi-Breader, padding well, covering them thoroughly. Repeat operation if heavier coating is desired. Fry in pan, in plenty of fat [if too little fat is used, breading will burn in spots], until brown. Remove; place in paper towel to remove surplus fat. Place cutlets in baking pan, sprinkle with a little melted butter, set into hot oven, and leave until well done. Serve 3 cutlets on medium platter with kitchenspoon of spaghetti. Breakfast plate for service. Garnish with parsley. Table d'hôte: serve 2 cutlets on breakfast plate with spoonful of spaghetti.

SPAGHETTI: Cook in boiling salted water until done.

MILANAISE SAUCE: Sauté in small sauce pan with a little butter, some chopped cold boiled tongue, ham, and mushrooms. Add well drained boiled spaghetti [in short lengths]. Add enough Spaghetti Italienne sauce to cover, sprinkle with a little grated cheese, let simmer until hot. [Order Spaghetti Italienne sauce from commissary.]

BREADED VEAL CUTLETS, SPAGHETTI ITALIENNE: Same as Breaded Veal Cutlets, Milanaise, except serve with a kitchenspoon of plain boiled spaghetti. Garnish with parsley. NOTE: Italienne Sauce should not be mixed into spaghetti, but a spoonful of sauce should be placed on top of spaghetti.

SPAGHETTI: Cook in boiling salted water until done.

ITALIENNE SAUCE:

2 Tablespoons Oil
1 medium onion, chopped
1 garlic clove, chopped
1 [6-ounce] can tomato paste
2 [28 ounce] cans crushed tomatoes
21 ounces water
¼ teaspoon salt
¼ teaspoon ground black pepper
1 teaspoon parsley

In the skillet, heat the oil, add the onion and garlic and saute for approximately 2 minutes. Add the tomato paste and cook on medium heat for 3 minutes, stirring constantly. Fill the empty tomato paste can full of water, add to the skillet, and cook for 1 minute, stirring. Remove from heat and set aside.

In an 8-quart saucepan, add the crushed tomatoes and cook on medium heat for 5 minutes. Fill the empty ground tomato can 3/4 full of water and add to the saucepan, along with the tomato paste mixture from the skillet. Mix thoroughly. Add the salt, ground pepper, and parsley and cook on medium heat for 15 minutes, then cover and cook on low heat for 2 1/2 hours, stirring every 15 minutes to prevent sticking and burning on bottom of pan.

BREADED VEAL CUTLETS, TOMATO SAUCE: Same as Breaded Veal Cutlets, Milanaise, except serve cutlets on medium platter resting in tomato sauce. Garnish with parsley. Breakfast plate for service. Table d'hôte: serve on breakfast plate.

TOMATO SAUCE: Use canned tomato soup, which you will use just as it comes out of the can for tomato sauce. Heat and serve.

BOILED SMOKED BEEF TONGUE, SPINACH: Put tongue in cold water to boil. Bring to boil then let simmer until done. Plunge into cold water and peel. Serve 4 good sized slices on bed of spinach on medium platter, breakfast plate for service. Garnish with parsley. Table d'hôte: serve on breakfast plate. NOTE: When canned tongue is furnished, just heat and serve as above.

SPINACH: Use canned spinach.

BROILED BACON, FRIED POTATOES: Serve 6 slices of bacon, broiled or fried as desired by guest, on medium platter, a strip of toast between each slice. Garnish with parsley. Bacon should be prepared in small amounts so it will be fresh in appearance when served. Breakfast plate for service. Table d'hôte: serve on breakfast plate.

FRIED POTATOES: Take boiled potatoes, slice and fry until brown; serve a liberal portion on platter with bacon.

BROILED HAM, FRIED POTATOES: Serve 1 slice of ham, broiled or fried as desired by guest, on medium platter with a liberal portion of fried potatoes. Garnish with parsley. Breakfast plate for service. Table d'hôte: serve on breakfast plate.

FRIED POTATOES: Same as Broiled Bacon, Fried Potatoes.

CHARCOAL BROILED SPECIAL SIRLOIN STEAK: Serve not less than 14 ounces, broiled as desired by guest, on medium platter.

Garnish with parsley and a slice of lemon, which has been dipped in paprika. French-fried potatoes around steak. 6 pieces. Place platter in front of guest, no service plate to be used. Serrated blade knife for service.

COLD BAKED HAM AND CHEESE, POTATO SALAD: Serve on medium platter an AD cup mold of potato salad, 2 slices of tomato. Serve two half slices of cold ham and one slice of cheese underlined with lettuce leaves. Discretion should be used as to the number of pieces of meat to be served according to size of slices. Garnish with parsley and slice of dill pickle. Cold breakfast plate for service. Table d'hôte: serve on breakfast plate.

POTATO SALAD: Same as Assorted Cold Cuts, Potato Salad.

COLD BAKED HAM AND TONGUE, POTATO SALAD: Same as Cold Baked Ham and Cheese, Potato Salad, except serve two slices of tongue instead of cheese.

POTATO SALAD: Same as Assorted Cold Cuts, Potato Salad.

CREAMED HAM AND CHICKEN, A LA KING: [Ingredients for about 6 orders]

1 kitchenspoon melted butter or chicken fat
1 boiled fowl, skinned and boned
4 cups diced, cooked ham, using ham hocks for this
2 green peppers, cut into 1" pieces, then blanched
1 small can mushrooms [pieces and stems]
1 can pimentoes [drained, dried, and cut into 1" slices]
2 cups medium thick cream sauce
½ cup sweet cream and 2 egg yolks, beaten together

PREPARATION: Sauté mushrooms and green peppers in the butter or fat for five minutes. Add chicken and ham meat, cut into ½ inch dice, then cream sauce and let simmer until well heated. Season with salt and then add the mixture of cream and eggs and at last the pimentoes. Shake well until properly mixed and bring to boiling point only. Sauce will curdle if left boiling. Serve on toast in casserole underlined with tea plate and doily. Breakfast plate for service. Garnish with parsley. Table d'hôte: same as A La Carte.

FRIED CALF LIVER WITH BACON OR ONION RINGS: Serve 3 pieces calf liver when slices are large, 4 pieces when slices are small, and 2 strips bacon or liberal portion French fried onion rings on medium platter as the case may be. Garnish with parsley. Do not put onions on liver. Liver should be dusted with flour before frying. Table d'hôte: serve on breakfast plate 2 pieces of calf liver if slices large or 3 pieces if slices are small.

FRENCH FRIED ONIONS: Onions should be sliced and then separated into rings. All except small center rings should be dipped into egg wash, then into flour, and fried a nice brown. Little center rings can be used in potato salad, etc.

BROILED PORK CHOPS, SPICED APPLE: Two chops about ¾ inch thick. Stripe on broiler and finish broiling in pan until done. When about half done, season with salt and pepper, serve on breakfast plate with two halves or one whole spiced apple, garnished with parsley. Serve on breakfast plate Table d'hôte and A La Carte.

[SPICED APPLE will come in #2½ size glass jars. Order as needed from Commissary. #10 size cans will have to be used until #2½ size jars are furnished]

SOUTHERN ROAST BEEF HASH: [To make ½ gallon of beef hash]

INGREDIENTS:

1 qt. diced roast beef
1 cup diced green peppers
1 cup diced onions
2 cups diced cooked white potatoes
1 tablespoonful of chicken base
½ teaspoon salt
¼ teaspoon white pepper
½ teaspoon paprika

1 cup flour
½ cup butter or bacon fat
3 cups of beef broth or consommé

PREPARATION: Sauté onions and green peppers until done in butter or bacon fat. Do not brown or burn the vegetable. Add flour; stir until mixed in. Add beef broth or consommé, beef and vegetables. Let cook for 3 to 5 minutes.

Serve on breakfast plate with one poached egg on top, garnish with parsley.

FRIED PORK CHOPS, APPLE RINGS: Chops about ¾" thick. Season with salt and pepper. Fry in pan until brown. Remove; place in paper towel to remove surplus fat. Serve on medium platter, resting on apple rings. Breakfast plate for service. Garnish with parsley. Table d'hôte: serve on breakfast plate.

APPLE RINGS: Core large baking apples carefully. Cut into 1/2 inch slices. Place in frying pan and fry.

GRILLED HAM STEAK, PINEAPPLE FRITTERS: One full cut of ham ¼ inch thick. Grilled. Use canned sliced pineapple.

PINEAPPLE FRITTER:
1 cup flour
1 teaspoon baking powder
¼ teaspoon salt
1 teaspoon powdered sugar
1 teaspoon melted butter
1 egg
milk

PREPARATION: Sift dry ingredients together in a mixing bowl. Break egg into center. Add some milk. Stir and gradually add enough milk until a fairly thick batter is obtained. Beat until all lumps have been removed. Stir in the melted butter. Dip pineapple into batter until well coated, and fry in deep, hot grease until browned. Drain fritters on a clean paper towel.

SERVICE: Serve on hot medium platter with pineapple fritter on same plate. Garnish with parsley. Breakfast plate for service. Table d'hôte: serve on dinner plate.

GRILLED LAMB CHOPS, BACON: 2 chops to order, single rib from 1 large end of rack or 2 chops from 3 ribs from small end of rack, resting on ½ piece of toast, with a slice of bacon on top of each chop. Chop frill on bone. Garnish with parsley. Serve on medium platter, breakfast plate for service. Table d'hôte: serve on breakfast plate.

GRILLED LAMB CHOPS, ON TOAST: Same as Grilled Lamb Chops, Bacon, except no bacon to be placed on chops.

OLD FASHIONED BEEF STEW-VEGETABLES:

Ingredients:

6 lbs. beef cut into squares 2-inch cubes
6 oz. fat from beef
4 diced onions
2 cups diced celery
4 tablespoons of flour
2 lbs. potatoes cut in inch squares
2 cups diced carrots
2 cups diced turnips
1 cup green peas
2 cups tomato puree

PREPARATION: Place meat which has been cut in 2 inch squares in a sauce pan seasoned with salt and pepper, simmer with fat, onions, and celery. When brown add 4 tablespoons of flour and simmer again. Then cover meat with water and boil, covered, until tender, about 1 or 1½ hours. Add potatoes, carrots, and turnips. Leave on fire until vegetables are soft; add tomato puree, peas, and cook until thoroughly heated.

SERVICE: Serve in casserole underlined with doily and tea plate. Breakfast plate for service. Sprinkle with chopped parsley. Table d'hôte service same as A La Carte.

Note: Order stew beef from the commissary by the pound.

OLD-FASHIONED BEEF POT PIE, EN CASSEROLE: Same as Old Fashioned Beef Stew-Vegetables except place in casserole with top crust and place in oven and brown.

SERVICE: Serve casserole underlined with doily and tea plate. Breakfast plate for service. Table d'hôte service same as A La Carte.

PIE CRUST RECIPE: Same as Deep Dish Apple Pie.

OUR OWN COUNTRY SAUSAGE WITH BOSTON BAKED BEANS: Serve one individual 7 oz. can of baked beans in a casserole underlined with doily and tea plate, and serve 2 cakes of sausage on top of baked beans, garnish with parsley. Breakfast plate for service. Table d'hôte: Serve on breakfast plate.

APPLE RINGS: Core large baking apples carefully. Cut into ½ inch slices. Place in frying pan and fry.

PRIME RIB OF BEEF NATURAL: Serve on hot medium platter. Garnish with parsley. Beef to be cut hot. Breakfast plate and serrated blade knife for service. Table d'hôte: serve on dinner plate.

PREPARATION: If not cut off, saw off chine bone and short ribs. Tie carefully, season with salt and pepper, place in roasting pan, fat side up. Use no vegetables when cooking roast. Roast should be frequently basted. Roast beef should be wrapped in greased brown paper for re-heating and when thoroughly reheated, placed in warming oven. COOKS MUST ALWAYS CARRY BROWN PAPER.

After roast has been removed from pan, pour off all clear fat, set pan on top of range, and let residue of meat juice cook down until very brown and sticking to bottom of pan. Add to pan for 5-rib roast, 1 qt.

water; for a 3-rib roast, 1 pint. Let come to boil and cook until residue has been loosened, strain through a clean white towel, which has been wrung out in cold water, into a quart crock, and keep hot. Pour 2 spoonfuls of juice over beef.

ROAST LEG OF LAMB, MINT SAUCE: Leg of lamb should weigh 6 to 8 pounds to the leg.

PREPARATION: Remove bones, tie leg, roast in roasting pan, pouring over it a little clean grease. Baste frequently while roasting, until done. Serve 2 or 3 pieces on medium platter. Breakfast plate for service. Garnish with parsley. Serve mint sauce in sauce boat. Table d'hôte: serve on breakfast plate.

MINT SAUCE: Pick leaves from bunch of fresh mint. Wash and chop very fine. Add to one cup of water, one cup sugar and one cup vinegar. Bring to boil and cook 15 minutes. Then strain through clean cloth into crock. When serving, add chopped fresh mint leaves.

ROAST LOIN OF PORK, APPLE SAUCE: Use pork loin. Sprinkle the meat with salt and pepper. Dust lightly with flour and roast. Place several small onions around the roast when cooking. Have the oven very hot the first 15 minutes and then cook in a medium oven slowly, allowing about 25 minutes to the pound. Roast should be frequently basted. Make gravy using equal amounts of fat and flour, adding about ½ as much hot water. Season with salt and pepper. Serve liberal portion of pork on medium platter, gravy on same. Garnish with parsley. Serve #45 ramekin of apple sauce on same plate. Breakfast plate for service. Table d'hôte: serve on breakfast plate.

APPLE SAUCE: Order from commissary.

SALISBURY STEAK, TOMATO SAUCE: Serve on medium platter, resting in tomato sauce. Garnish with parsley, breakfast plate for service. Table d'hôte: serve on breakfast plate.

PREPARATION: [Ingredients for 4 portions]

2 cups finely ground beef
½ cup cream
1 small onion, washed, minced, and sautéed
½ cup breadcrumbs
1 egg
salt and pepper

Mix ingredients well, mixing a small amount at a time, keeping very cold; form into oblong steaks, fry until brown.

TOMATO SAUCE: Use canned tomato soup, which you will use just as it comes out of the can for tomato sauce. Heat and serve.

SALISBURY STEAK, MUSHROOM SAUCE: Same as Salisbury Steak, Tomato Sauce.

MUSHROOM SAUCE:

3 tablespoons butter
3 tablespoons flour
1 teaspoon beef stock
8 oz. can mushrooms, stems and pieces
few drops onion juice
1 cup milk
salt and paprika

Brown the butter, onion juice and flour. Pour over cream gradually, stirring constantly. Add chopped mushrooms, which have been sautéed in butter. Season with beef stock, salt, and paprika.

HAMBURGER STEAK, TOMATO SAUCE: Same as Salisbury Steak, Tomato Sauce.

HAMBURGER STEAK, MUSHROOM SAUCE: Same as Salisbury Steak, Mushroom Sauce.

BEEF STROGANOFF, SOUTHERN:

2 lb beef slices, browned in fat

1 cup mushrooms
1 cup tomato soup
1 onion, chopped
1½ cups water

After browning beef, cook in mixture of other ingredients for 1½ hours. Stir in 1 cup sour cream before serving.

COUNTRY STEAK, BROWN GRAVY: Steaks will come cut 3 to the pound and you will order by the pound as needed. Dredge with flour and brown slowly on both sides in fat in skillet. Sprinkle with 1/3 teaspoon salt for each steak and a dash of pepper, add water and cover and simmer over very low heat until meat is tender. Add a small amount of additional water during cooking period if needed. Thicken gravy with a paste of flour and water. Use 2 teaspoons flour for each cup of juice and drippings. Add flour and water paste to liquid after meat has been removed from skillet. Water may be added to make enough gravy, stir until gravy thickens and serve two country steaks resting on gravy on medium platter. Breakfast plate for service. Garnish with parsley. Table d'hôte: serve one steak on breakfast plate.

HAM AND CABBAGE: Use hocks and ends of hams that have been boiled until done. Cabbage: Take off outside leaves and cut heads into ¼, 1/6, or 1/8 depending on size of head. Remove the tough core. Cook uncovered in salted boiling water for 15 to 20 minutes. Drain and serve wedge of cabbage with liberal amount of ham on medium platter. Breakfast plate for service. Garnish with parsley. Table d'hôte: serve on breakfast plate.

CLUB STEAK: We will use top sirloin butt which will weigh around 12 to 15 pounds each. Order a whole or half as needed. Be sure to cut steak across the grain, approximately 12-ounce steaks to be served. Broil as desired by guest on charcoal broiler. Serve on medium platter; garnish with 6 pieces of French fried potatoes, parsley, and slice of lemon. [NOTE: Cut a full slice across the grain and cut thick enough so that when slice is large, you can cut in half and serve a smaller thick slice than a large thin slice.]

BREADED PORK CHOPS, APPLE SAUCE: Chops about ½ inch thick. Season with salt and pepper. Pour some Redi-Breader in shallow pan or dish. Moisten well the pork chops to be breaded and roll them in Redi-Breader, padding well, covering them thoroughly. Repeat operation if heavier coating is desired. Fry in pan, in plenty of fat [if too little is used, breading will burn in spots] until brown. Remove; place in paper towel to remove surplus fat. Place chops in baking pan, sprinkle with a little melted butter, set into hot oven and leave until well done. Serve on medium platter with #47 ramekin of apple sauce on same platter. Use canned apple sauce for this service. Garnish with parsley. Breakfast plate for service. Table d'hôte: serve on breakfast plate.

APPLE SAUCE: Order from commissary.

COMBINATION GRILL: Serve one lamb chop resting on ½ slice of toast with a slice of bacon on top of chop. Chop frill on bone. One slice of grilled calf liver and ½ slice of grilled ham. Garnish with parsley and serve on hot breakfast plate. Serrated steak knife for service.

HAM CROQUETTES, CREAM SAUCE: Use hock and ends of ham. Boil and mince. Use two parts ham and one part mashed potatoes. Mix and add egg yolks and season with a little pepper. Form into cone shape and dip into egg wash and then Redi-Breader and fry in deep grease. On A La Carte serve three croquettes on medium platter, breakfast plate for service. On Table d'hôte serve two croquettes on breakfast plate. Garnish with parsley.

BAKED MEAT LOAF, TOMATO SAUCE: [ON COMBINATION MEAL FLYER] Serve two slices about ½ inch thick resting in tomato sauce on compartment plate or dinner plate. Garnish with parsley. Choice of two vegetables on same plate.

3 lbs. ground beef
Add ½ lb. sausage
1 cup cream
2 eggs, well beaten
2 teaspoons salt

½ teaspoon pepper
2 cups bread crumbs
1 cup onions, finely chopped and sautéed

Mix well and place into greased baking pan and bake in moderately hot oven for 45 minutes.

TOTMATO SAUCE: Use canned tomato soup just as it comes from the can. Heat and serve.

BRAISED BEEF, VEGETABLES:

INGREDIENTS:

6 pounds meat
8 oz. fat from beef
2 cups diced onions
4 cups diced potatoes
2 cups diced carrots
1 cup diced turnips
1 cup green peas
2 cups tomato sauce

Use boneless beef or trim lean beef from rib ends. Dredge with flour and brown slowly in fat in skillet, season with salt and pepper. Place in iron roasting pan and cover. Add a small amount of water and braise in very slow oven until meat is tender and then last 45 minutes of cooking period add vegetables and tomato sauce except peas. Add peas last 5 minutes. Add small amount of water if needed during cooking period. Serve in casserole underlined with tea plate and doily. Garnish with sprig of parsley on top of casserole, breakfast plate for service.

BRAISED RIB ENDS OF BEEF, VEGETABLES: Trim surplus fat from short ribs. Place in roasting pan. Season with salt and pepper and put in oven. Turn from time to time so they will cook evenly. When half done, add some carrots, onions, and celery. When about ¾ done, remove short ribs from pan and add some water to juice and make a gravy. During cooking, skim off excess grease occasionally.

Place ribs back in pan and finish cooking. Remove ribs to platter and put gravy in crock and let stand until grease floats so it may be skimmed from gravy. Serve liberal portion on compartment plate in gravy, with choice of two vegetables. Garnish with parsley.

REBEL BREAKFAST $1.50-CRISP STREAK-O-LEAN BACON WITH ONE EGG, GRITS WITH CREAM GRAVY:

FRUIT, JUICE, OR CEREAL: Same as Table d'hôte.

PREPARATION: It is noticed that cooks are not preparing this breakfast properly. First, this salt bacon must be cut in thin slices, then cut slits in the rind so that the meat will not curl, and parboil. The parboil must be started in cold water. Fry the bacon on top of the range to a golden brown.

CREAM GRAVY:

1 teaspoon flour
½ pint sweet mink
Pinch salt
Tablespoon fat

Place fat and flour in pan, brown, add milk and stir until smooth.

SERVICE: Serve three slices of streaked meat with one egg on breakfast plate, garnished with parsley. Serve cream gravy on side in gravy boat and grits in fruit saucer. Egg should be prepared any style requested by patron.

THESE INSTRUCTIONS MUST BE STRICTLY ADHERED TO AND UNDER NO CONDITIONS WILL COOK FRY THIS BACON WITHOUT FIRST PARBOILING IT. DO NOT CUT RIND OFF AND DO NOT BREAD THIS BACON.

LAMB CHOPS DINNER: 2 chops to order, single rib from large end of rack or 2 chops from 3 ribs from small end of rack, resting on ½ piece of toast, with a slice of bacon on top of each chop. Chop frill on bone. Garnish with parsley. Serve on breakfast plate.

SOUP OR JUICE: Same as A La Carte.

CHOICE OF TWO VEGETABLES: Serve in bakers on side.

HEAD LETTUCE, FRENCH DRESSING: ¼ or 1/6 head of lettuce, depending on size of head, on tea plate with French dressing poured over same.

BREAD: 2 hot rolls, 1 white and 1 whole wheat, on tea plate underlined with doily. Pat of butter in butter chip. We will use half baked rolls, which should be browned in oven and served hot. Brown only a few rolls at a time.

DESSERT: Same as Table d'hôte.

BEVERAGE: Same as Table d'hôte.

SOUTHERN BARBECUE RIBS:

Cook ribs in a slow oven for three to four hours, until tender, basting occasionally with Southern Barbecue Sauce. Serve 1/3 to ½ rack, depending on size, serrated knife for service.

GRILLED STEAK SOUTHERN STYLE:

Take one, 8 to 10 ounce Strip Steak. Liberally sprinkle with salt and pepper on both sides, taking time to press it into the meat. Cook to order on grill. Garnish with parsley. Serve on dinner plate. Serrated knife for service.

VEGETABLE STUFFED PORK CHOPS:

4 pork chops, about 1-inch thick
3 tablespoons butter
1 small zucchini, finely diced
1 red bell pepper, finely diced
1 yellow pepper, finely diced
1 yellow onion, finely diced

Salt and black pepper
2 tablespoons minced garlic
1/4 teaspoon red pepper flakes
½ cup ketchup
½ cup balsamic vinegar

Heat the oil in a large sauté pan over high heat. Add the zucchini, peppers, onion and salt and pepper, to taste, and cook until almost soft, 5 minutes. Stir in the garlic and the red pepper flakes and cook for 30 seconds. Set aside to cool.

Cut a pocket in the pork chops going almost completely through. Stuff the vegetable mix into the pocket, secure with a toothpick [there will be vegetables left over]. Add a little more butter to the pan if necessary, reheat over medium heat, and place the chops in the pan, turning them about every 5 minutes. Cook for a total of 25-30 minutes. Remove from pan and place on plate to rest.

Add balsamic vinegar and ketchup to the pan drippings, stirring constantly for 3-4 minutes. Pour sauce over chops and garnish with remaining vegetables.

PORK CHOPS, PAN GRAVY:

4 Pork chops, about 1 inch thick
2 Tablespoons butter
1½ Cups white wine
Flour

Melt butter in frying pan. Fry pork chops slowly, turning several times to avoid burning, until done and golden brown in color. Remove chops and place on plate, cover with foil to keep warm.

Wisk 1-2 tablespoons of flour into pan drippings to make a roux, stirring constantly. Add the wine to the pan. Wisk constantly to keep lumps from forming until gravy thickens. Remove from heat.

Serve one chop per order, topped with 1-2 tablespoons of the gravy.

Atlanta, Ga., January 30, 1956

File 5/210

ALL DINING CAR STEWARDS AND CHEFS:

    On diners that are serving country ham, either on the breakfast or on the dinner meal, this country ham should be rinsed thoroughly in cold water. If the ham is extremely salty it should be parboiled a few minutes in the frying pan before frying.

E. L. Frapart

Superintendent, Dining Cars

Cc: All concerned.

OMELETS

CHOPPED HAM OMELET: Make omelet with 3 eggs. Add a small amount of milk, whip thoroughly, and add a liberal portion of cooked, chopped ham, using ham hock or end of ham, to this mixture. Garnish with parsley. Serve on medium platter. On Club Breakfast, use two eggs. Table d'hôte: use 2 eggs, serve on breakfast plate.

OMELET WITH CHEESE: Make omelet, using 3 eggs, whipping thoroughly, adding a little milk. Place in a greased omelet pan, and after eggs have begun to set sprinkle one tablespoon of chopped or grated American cheese, then fold into shape of an omelet. Serve on medium platter, breakfast plate for service. Garnish with parsley. On Club Breakfast, use two eggs. Table d'hôte: use 2 eggs, serve on breakfast plate.

OMELET WITH FRESH TOMATOES: Make omelet with 3 eggs, add a little milk and whip thoroughly. When done, place a spoonful of stewed tomatoes in center and fold. Place another spoonful of tomatoes in front of omelet, on medium platter. Breakfast plate for service. Garnish with parsley. Use 2 eggs for Table d'hôte, serve on breakfast plate.

PLAIN OMELET: Take 2 eggs, add a small amount of milk and whip thoroughly. When done, fold in shape of omelet. Serve on medium platter. Garnish with parsley, one slice of tomato, and 4 French fried potatoes.

POULTRY LIVER OR CHICKEN LIVER OMELET: Cut 3 blanched chicken livers into 12 pieces, and sauté for a few minutes, then add sufficient espagnola sauce and simmer for 5 minutes. Make omelet with 3 eggs, add a small amount of milk and whip thoroughly. When done, place a spoonful of chicken liver mixture in center and fold. Place another spoonful of mixture in front of omelet. Serve on medium platter, breakfast plate for service. Garnish with parsley. On Club Breakfast, use two eggs. Table d'hôte: use 2 eggs, serve on breakfast plate. Garnish with parsley.

SPANISH OMELET: Make omelet with 3 eggs, add small amount of milk and whip thoroughly. When done, place a spoonful of Spanish sauce in center and fold. Place another spoonful of sauce in front of omelet on medium platter. Garnish with parsley, breakfast plate for service. Use 2 eggs on Club Breakfast. Table d'hôte: use 2 eggs, serve on breakfast plate.

SPANISH SAUCE: Sauté together in a sauce pan with a little butter, ½ teaspoon paprika, 1 cup each sliced onions, green peppers, and mushrooms until soft. Add 3 cups canned stewed tomatoes. Season with salt, 1 teaspoon sugar. Let simmer until thick, use no flour to thicken this sauce, but reduce to proper consistency.

BACON OMELET: Make omelet with 3 eggs. Add a small amount of milk, whip thoroughly add a liberal portion of cooked chopped bacon to this mixture. Make into form of omelet. Serve on medium platter. On Club Breakfast, use two eggs. Table d'hôte: use 2 eggs, serve on breakfast plate.

RELISHES A LA CARTE

CANDIED DILL STRIPS: Serve liberal portion candied dill strips in fruit saucer underlined with lettuce leaves.

CRISP CELERY: Serve crisp celery in large celery tray with crushed ice. 6 quarter stalks.

MIXED OLIVES: Serve 2 green, 2 stuffed, and 3 ripe olives in fruit saucer underlined with lettuce leaf and covered with crushed ice.

OLIVES: Serve 5 or 6 olives in fruit saucer, underlined with lettuce leaf and covered with crushed ice.

RADISHES: 6 or 7 radishes to be rose-budded. Serve in fruit saucer underlined with lettuce leaf.

SLICED TOMATOES: Serve 5 slices of tomato overlapping each other on lettuce leaves on tea plate. 4 flake cracker on tea plate underlined with doily or 1 individual package. Serve dressing as desired in gravy boat.

SWEET GHERKINS: Serve six to eight gherkins in fruit saucer, underlined with lettuce leaf.

SWEET PICKLES: Serve liberal portion sweet mixed pickles or 6 small whole sweet pickles in fruit saucer underlined with lettuce leaf.

SWEET PICKLE CHIPS: Serve liberal portion sweet pickle chips in fruit saucer underlined with lettuce leaf.

RELISHES TABLE D'HOTE

CANDIED DILL STRIPS: Serve liberal portion candied dill strips in fruit saucer underlined with lettuce leaves.

CRISP CELERY: Two quarter stalks, cut tops short, in individual celery tray, covered with crushed ice. Celery should be cut so there will not be too much overlap in tray.

CELERY AND OLIVES: Two quarter stalks celery, cut tops short, and 2 olives in individual celery tray, covered with crushed ice. Celery should be cut so there will not be too much overlap in tray.

MIXED OLIVES: Serve 2 green, 2 ripe, and 1 stuffed olive in fruit saucer underlined with lettuce leaf and covered with crushed ice.

RADISHES AND OLIVES: Serve two olives and two radishes to be rose-budded in fruit saucer underlined with lettuce leaf.

SWEET GHERKINS: Serve 3 gherkins in fruit saucer, underlined with lettuce leaf.

SWEET PICKLES: Serve liberal portion sweet mixed pickles or 3 small whole sweet pickles in fruit saucer underlined with lettuce leaf.

SWEET PICKLE CHIPS: Serve liberal portion sweet pickle chips in fruit saucer underlined with lettuce leaves.

SALADS A LA CARTE

CHICKEN SALAD, CRACKERS: Preparation same as for Chicken Salad Sandwich. Serve a coffee cup mold of chicken salad in oatmeal bowl underlined with lettuce leaf, top with a dessert spoon of mayonnaise. Garnish with 2 strips of pimentos in the form of a cross [X] and a whole hard boiled egg, quartered. 4 flake crackers on tea plate underlined with doily, or 1 individual package of crackers. Tea plate for service. Durkees dressing on side in original container.

HEAD LETTUCE: Serve ½ head lettuce cut into 2 pieces in oatmeal bowl, underlined with doily and tea plate, another tea plate for service. Crackers on tea plate. Dressing as desired in gravy boat.

LETTUCE AND GRAPEFRUIT SALAD: Serve slice of lettuce about 1" thick with 5 sections of grapefruit on top of same on tea plate. French dressing on side in gravy boat.

LETTUCE AND PINEAPPLE SALAD: Serve slice of lettuce about 1" thick with two rings of pineapple placed on it, on tea plate. French dressing in gravy boat.

LETTUCE AND TOMATO SALAD: Serve ½ head lettuce and 3 slices tomato in oatmeal bowl underlined with doily and tea plate. Another tea plate for service. Dressing in gravy boat, as desired. 4 flake crackers on tea plate underlined with doily, or 1 individual package crackers. ALL INGREDIENTS FOR SALAD MUST BE THOROUGHLY CHILLED. ALL DRESSING MUST BE KEPT CHILLED.

TOMATO STUFFED WITH CHICKEN SALAD: Preparation of chicken salad same as for Chicken Salad Sandwich. Use large tomato if possible, and if not use two medium tomatoes. Hollow inside of tomato from stem end. Stuff with chicken salad, garnish top of chicken salad with two slices pimentos in form of cross [X]. Serve on chilled breakfast plate on bed of lettuce leaves. Garnish with two slices dill pickle and two olives. Two individual packages crackers on tea plate.

SOUTHERN SALAD BOWL: Lettuce leaves, cut or shredded into small pieces. Celery, properly stringed and cut crosswise in slices of about ¼ inch thick. If celery branch is large, it should be split lengthwise first. Radishes, washed clean and sliced thinly crosswise. Do not peel. Cucumbers, peeled and cut into about ¼ inch dice. Tomatoes cut in triangular pieces, similar to orange sections, do not slice. Green peppers, remove seeds and slice about 3 rings about 1/8 inch thick and cut into small pieces.

All of the above to be placed together in salad bowl and mixed lightly. Pour French dressing over all ingredients.

All items for salad bowl must not be mixed ahead but each salad bowl must be made at time of service so that it will be fresh and crisp.

If the order is given by one person, use the smaller bowl, which should contain ingredients for one person. If service is desired by 2 or more persons, use larger bowl, having it contain enough ingredients for the number of people ordering. A fork and spoon should be placed in bowl for service. A tea plate should also be supplied for each person ordering salad.

Full price to be charged trainmen wanting this service.

This salad bowl should be made as attractive as possible.

Serve 2 double flake crackers or Ry-Krisp on tea plate underlined with doily or 1 individual package of flake crackers. ALL INGREDIENTS FOR SALAD MUST BE THOROUGHLY CHILLED. ALL DRESSINGS MUST BE KEPT CHILLED.

SALADS TABLE D'HOTE

CHILLED BROCCOLI SALAD:

1 head Broccoli
1 medium onion, chopped
1 can mushroom pieces, drained
Italian Dressing

Combine first three ingredients in a bowl. Add Italian dressing until barely covered. Cover, place in chill box. Allow to marinate 6-8 hours before serving. Serve 1 to 2 kitchenspoonfuls in fruit saucer.

COMBINATION SALAD, FRENCH DRESSING: Into crock place shredded lettuce, raw carrot thinly sliced, celery and wedges of tomatoes, mix lightly. Serve a kitchenspoon full of the above mixture in oatmeal bowl; top same with ring of raw onion and a ring of green pepper. DO NOT UNDERLINE THE OATMEAL BOWL WITH TEA PLATE. French dressing poured over same in pantry. ALL INGREDIENTS FOR SALAD MUST BE THOROUGHLY CHILLED. ALL DRESSING MUST BE CHILLED.

HEAD LETTUCE, THOUSAND ISLAND DRESSING: Serve ¼ or 1/6 head lettuce, depending on size of head, on tea plate. Dressing poured over.

THOUSAND ISLAND DRESSING: [Ingredients for 1 quart]

2 hard boiled eggs, yolks and whites chopped fine
2 green peppers, chopped, but not too fine
2 pimentos, chopped, but not too fine
1½ cups mayonnaise
1 cup chili sauce

Mix ingredients together in mixing bowl with egg whip. Transfer to quart jar, cover tightly. Keep in chill box.

LETTUCE AND GRAPEFRUIT SALAD: Serve slice of lettuce about 1" thick with 3 sections of grapefruit on top of same on tea plate. Pour French dressing over salad in pantry. ALL INGREDIENTS FOR SALAD MUST BE THOROUGHLY CHILLED. ALL DRESSING MUST BE CHILLED.

LETTUCE AND PINEAPPLE SALAD: Serve slice of lettuce about 1" thick with a ring of pineapple placed on it, on tea plate. Pour French dressing over salad in pantry. ALL INGREDIENTS FOR SALAD MUST BE THOROUGHLY CHILLED. ALL DRESSING MUST BE CHILLED.

LETTUCE AND TOMATO SALAD: Serve ¼ head lettuce and 2 slices tomato on tea plate. Pour French dressing over salad in pantry. ALL INGREDIENTS FOR SALAD MUST BE THOROUGHLY CHILLED. ALL DRESSING MUST BE CHILLED.

LETTUCE AND TOMATO SALAD, VINAIGRETTE: Same as Lettuce and Tomato Salad, except Vinaigrette sauce poured over salad in pantry.

VINAGRETTE SAUCE:

1 onion, washed and chopped fine
1 dill pickle, washed and chopped fine
1 tablespoon parsley, washed and chopped fine
1 hard boiled egg, whites and yolks chopped fine and separated
1½ cups French dressing

Mix all ingredients together. ALL INGREDIENTS FOR SALAD MUST BE THOROUGHLY CHILLED. ALL DRESSING MUST BE CHILLED.

PRINCESS SALAD: Place on tea plate a bed of shredded lettuce. Place on lettuce 1 slice of tomato. On tomato, place 1 spear of asparagus. Place 1 thin strip of pimento across the asparagus. Place 1 dessert spoonful of vinaigrette sauce over same.

VINAGRETTE SAUCE: Same as Lettuce and Tomato, Vinaigrette.

SLICED TOMATOES, SOUTHERN: Serve 3 slices of tomato overlapping each other on lettuce leaves on tea plate. Liberal portion of Durkee's dressing poured over. ALL INGREDIENTS FOR SALAD MUST BE THOROUGHLY CHILLED. ALL DRESSING MUST BE CHILLED.

LETTUCE, PINEAPPLE, COTTAGE CHEESE SALAD: Serve on tea plate a bed of shredded lettuce with a ring of pineapple placed on it and a liberal portion of cottage cheese placed in hole of pineapple. French dressing poured over.

THE SALAD BOWL: The Salad Bowl that appears on the Crescent Dinner, Table d'hôte should be made as follows:

We will use our regular salad bowl ingredients and serve a liberal portion in an oatmeal bowl. Guests should be served their choice of dressing on this salad bowl which should be poured over the salad in the pantry.

Waiters should be careful to serve the exact dressing ordered by the guests.

TOSSED SALAD: Use head lettuce, endive, and romaine. Ratio of one bunch endive, one bunch romaine, to four heads of lettuce. Wash ingredients in cold water, thoroughly. Remove core from head lettuce and allow cold water to run into the opening. Shake to remove excess water. Tear, rather than cut, ingredients into small pieces, no larger than a half dollar coin. Place ingredients onto clean cloth [apron, etc., depending on amount to be used], toss about gently in cloth to mix and remove water. Place cloth containing salad into produce box to chill. Always make salad far enough in advance to be chilled before serving. Draw from chill box as needed.

Serve in oatmeal bowl, underlined with doily and tea plate. After meal service, salad is to be removed from cloth and placed in crock, covered, for storage in chill box.

SANDWICHES

CHEESE SANDWICH: Take 3 slices of bread, buttering the first slice, placing a slice of cheese on it. Set your second slice of bread on top of this, buttering same, then place another slice of cheese on the second slice of bread, then place the third slice of bread on top of this, thus making a double deck sandwich. Trim crust from bread. Cut sandwich diagonally, from corner to corner, that is sandwich will be cut into 4 diagonal sections. Place a toothpick through each section of sandwich to hold together. Serve on breakfast plate on lettuce leaf setting the 4 wedges of sandwich on end in star fashion. Garnish with a slice of tomato and a slice of dill pickle. Mustard on side in original container.

CHICKEN SALAD SANDWICH ON TOASTED BREAD: Use white and dark meat of boiled chicken. Chop chicken, add chopped celery and just enough mayonnaise to hold ingredients together. Chicken salad sandwich should consist of 3 layers of bread as desired by guest, mayonnaise and lettuce between 2 slices of bread and chicken salad between second and third slices of bread. Cut sandwich diagonally and serve on lettuce leaf on breakfast plate. Garnish sandwich by placing a slice of dill pickle on top of sandwich and a slice of tomato in front of sandwich in center of the plate facing guest. Toothpick through each section of sandwich to hold together. Durkee's dressing on side in original container.

CLUB SANDWICH: 3 slices of toasted bread, buttered on 1 side. On first slice of toast place 2 leaves of crisp fresh lettuce, on top of this place 2 slices of tomato, spread with mayonnaise, and place second piece of toast on this, buttered side up. Cover with sliced white meat of chicken and 2 slices of bacon on top of chicken. Place third piece of toast on top of bacon, buttered side down. Cut diagonally, putting toothpick through each section to hold together, placing an olive on top of each toothpick. Serve on medium platter, resting on lettuce leaf; garnish with a tomato, quartered, and a slice of dill pickle. Tea plate for service. Durkee's dressing on side in original container.

HAM SANDWICH: Take 3 slices of bread, buttering the first slice, placing a slice of ham on it. Set your second slice of bread on top of this, buttering same, then place another slice of ham on the second slice of bread, then place the third slice of bread on top of this, thus making a double deck sandwich. Trim crust from bread. Cut sandwich diagonally, from corner to corner, that is sandwich will be cut into 4 pieces. Place a toothpick through each section of sandwich to hold together. Serve on breakfast plate on lettuce leaf, setting the 4 wedges of sandwich on end in star fashion. Garnish with a slice of tomato and a slice of dill pickle. Mustard on side in original container.

HAM AND CHEESE SANDWICH: Take 3 slices of bread, buttering the first slice, placing a slice of ham on it. Set your second slice of bread on top of this, buttering same, then place a slice of cheese on the second slice of bread, then place the third slice of bread on top of this, thus making a double deck sandwich. Trim crust from bread. Cut sandwich diagonally, from corner to corner, that is sandwich will be cut into 4 pieces. Place a toothpick through each section of sandwich to hold together. Serve on breakfast plate on lettuce leaf, setting the 4 wedges of sandwich on end in star fashion. Garnish with a slice of tomato and a slice of dill pickle. Mustard on side in original container.

HAM AND EGG SANDWICH: Serve ½ slice fried ham on 1 piece toasted bread and a fried egg, fried on both sides, yellow broken, on the other slice of bread, on medium platter. This should be an open-faced sandwich. Garnish with slice of dill pickle. Breakfast plate for service.

LETTUCE AND TOMATO SANDWICH: Use 3 slices of bread, putting lettuce and tomato and mayonnaise between the two, cut sandwich diagonally and serve on lettuce leaf on breakfast plate, placing a slice of dill pickle on top of the sandwich. Toothpick through each section of sandwich to hold together.

SMOKED TONGUE SANDWICH: Take 3 slices of bread, buttering the first slice, placing a slice of tongue on it. Set your second slice of bread on top of this, buttering same, then place another slice of tongue on the second piece of bread, then place the third slice of bread on top of this, thus making a double deck sandwich. Trim crust from bread. Cut sandwich diagonally, from corner to corner, that is sandwich will be cut into 4 pieces. Place a toothpick through each section of sandwich to hold together. Serve on breakfast plate on lettuce leaf, setting the 4 wedges of sandwich on end in star fashion. Garnish with a slice of tomato and a slice of dill pickle. Mustard on side in original container.

SAUCES

CIDER SAUCE: [Ingredients for 1 quart]

1½ pt. beef stock [ham or chicken stock will do]
1 pt. apple juice
¼ teaspoon pepper
½ cup butter
1 teaspoon salt
¼ cup brown sugar
½ cup flour

Simmer 10 minutes until chestnut brown. Add hot stock and whip smooth.

CREAM SAUCE: [Ingredients for ½ gallon]

½ cup butter or chicken fat
1½ quarts boiling milk
1 cup flour
Salt

PREPARATION: Melt butter or chicken fat in sauce pan. Add flour and make a roux. Let cook at least 10 minutes to which add boiling milk gradually, stirring constantly with egg whip to prevent sauce getting lumpy. Cook 30 minutes. Season with salt only. Strain into crock and place small bits of butter on top to prevent crust forming.

LEMON BUTTER: Melt ½ pound butter and add juice of one lemon. Spread a tablespoon full over the fish.

MINT SAUCE: Pick leaves from bunch of fresh mint. Wash and chop very fine. Add to one cup of water, 1 cup sugar and 1 cup vinegar. Bring to boil and cook 15 minutes. Then strain through clean cloth into a crock. When serving, add chopped fresh mint leaves.

MUSHROOM SAUCE:

3 tablespoons butter
3 tablespoons flour
1 teaspoon beef stock
8 oz. can mushrooms, stems and pieces
few drops onion juice
1 cup milk
salt and paprika

Brown the butter, onion juice and flour. Pour over cream gradually, stirring constantly. Add chopped mushrooms, which have been sautéed in butter. Season with beef stock, salt, and paprika.

RAISIN SAUCE: To 1 quart of water, add 1 cup of blanched raisins, 1 teaspoon sugar, juice of 1/2 lemon and let come to boil. Then simmer for 10 minutes.

SOUTHERN BARBECUE SAUCE: [Ingredients for 5 gallons]

¾ cup chili powder
2 quarts bourbon
1 gallon beef stock
4 tablespoons salt
2 tablespoons cayenne pepper
1 case ketchup
4 cups cider vinegar
1 lb. butter
1 cup shallots, diced small
½ cup chopped garlic

1½ cups dry mustard
2 cups molasses
5 tablespoons ground black pepper
4 tablespoons white pepper
2 cups Worcestershire Sauce
1 #10 can chili sauce
10 lbs. brown sugar
2 bunches celery, diced
4 green peppers, diced

Sauté celery, shallots, garlic, and green pepper until shallots are transparent. Add bourbon and reduce by 2/3. Add all other ingredients, and steep but do not boil. Cook for one hour, stirring occasionally. Strain and cool.

SPANISH SAUCE: Sauté together in a sauce pan with a little butter, ½ teaspoon paprika, 1 cup each sliced onions, green peppers, and mushrooms until soft. Add 3 cups canned stewed tomatoes. Season with salt, 1 teaspoon sugar. Let simmer until thick, use no flour to thicken this sauce, but reduce to proper consistency.

TARTAR SAUCE:

1 qt. mayonnaise
½ bunch parsley, chopped very fine and squeezed dry
1 coffee cup dill pickles, chopped very fine and squeezed dry
2 onions, washed and chopped very fine
2 hard boiled eggs, whites and yolks separated, chopped fine

PREPARATION: Mix pickles, onions, parsley together in mixing bowl, add mayonnaise and stir well. Add chopped eggs. Keep in cool place. **Make fresh daily.** Note: Onions must not be run through food chopper, but must be chopped by hand.

THOUSAND ISLAND DRESSING: [Ingredients for 1 quart]

2 hard-boiled eggs, yolks and whites chopped fine
2 green peppers, chopped, but not too fine
2 pimentos, chopped, but not too fine
1½ cups mayonnaise
1 cup chili sauce

Mix ingredients together in mixing bowl with egg whip. Transfer to quart jar. Cover tightly. Keep in chill box.

TOMATO SAUCE: Use canned tomato soup, which you will use just as it comes out of the can for tomato sauce. Heat and serve.

LEMON SAUCE: Use prepared lemon pudding mixture, cutting the pudding to the proper consistency for a sauce.

VANILLA SAUCE: Use prepared vanilla pudding mixture, cutting the pudding to the proper consistency for a sauce.

SEAFOODS

<u>BROILED FRESH FISH, LEMON BUTTER</u>: Use 2 lb. fish [whatever market best affords]. Serve ½ to portion, if fish is large, use approximately half of a 2 lb. fish. Scale, trim, cut and remove bones and surplus fat. Pour a little oil on large platter. Dip fish into oil, sprinkle with paprika and broil with skin side up, over clean fire, until brown and done. At last minute, prior to removing fish, turn it over, placing skin side down, permitting it to remain long enough to crisp the skin; serve on medium platter. Garnish with 1/8 lemon and parsley. Breakfast plate for service. Serve on breakfast plate, Table d'hôte.

<u>LEMON BUTTER</u>: Melt ½ pound butter and add juice of one lemon. Spread a tablespoon full over this fish.

<u>CRAB IMPERIAL</u>:

1 lb. crab meat
well beaten
3 teaspoons mayonnaise
1 egg,

Mix all the ingredients together, add salt and pepper to taste. Fill crab shells with the mixture. Dot with butter or margarine. Brown in a hot oven [400 degrees] for 6 to 10 minutes. Makes three.

<u>FRIED FISH, TARTAR SAUCE</u>: Serve 2 or 3 pieces on hot medium platter, garnish with 1/8 lemon. Serve tartar sauce in #45 ramekin on same platter. Breakfast plate for service. Use whatever fish market best affords, using approximately half of a two pound fish. Cut into 2 or 3 pieces. Pour some Redi-Breader in shallow pan or dish. Roll the pieces of fish in Redi-Breader, padding well, covering them thoroughly. Fry in deep fat.

<u>TARTAR SAUCE</u>:

1 qt. mayonnaise
½ bunch parsley, chopped very fine and squeezed dry
1 coffee cup dill pickles, chopped very fine and squeezed dry

2 onions, washed and chopped very fine
2 hard boiled eggs, whites and yolks separated, chopped fine

PREPARATION: Mix pickles, onions, parsley together in mixing bowl, add mayonnaise and stir well. Add chopped eggs. Keep in cool place. **Make fresh daily.** Note: Onions must not be run through food chopper, but must be chopped by hand.

FRIED OYSTERS: Six [6] oysters on medium platter. Garnish with parsley, 1/8 lemon and slice of dill pickle and tartar sauce or chili sauce in #45 or 47 ramekin on same platter. Breakfast plate for service. Table d'hôte: serve on breakfast plate, five [5] oysters if large. If small use discretion.

PREPARATION: Follow directions that come in the 10 pound package of Redi-Breader, but in preparing oysters, you will not use water as oysters contain sufficient amount of moisture.

FRESH SHRIMP COCKTAIL: Take shrimp and remove the black vein from their backs and place in cold water about 30 minutes to make firm. Serve approximately six or eight shrimp depending on size, underlined with lettuce leaf, with cocktail sauce poured over same in stem cocktail glass underlined with tea plate and doily. Cocktail fork on right side of tea plate for service, and 1/8 lemon on left side of tea plate.

COCKTAIL SAUCE: One 14oz. bottle of catsup mixed with one tablespoon of horseradish.

IMPORTED SARDINES, CRACKERS: Open the can of sardines with a can opener. Serve opened can on small platter on lettuce leaf. Garnish with ¼ lemon. Oyster fork on platter. Tea plate for service. Crackers. Table d'hôte: serve on breakfast plate.

COLD IMPORTED SARDINES, HARD BOILED EGG, SLICED CRACKERS: Serve on cold medium platter can of sardines opened with can opener underlined with lettuce leaves in center of platter. Serve one whole, quartered, hard-boiled egg on one end of the platter underlined with lettuce leaves and 3 slices of tomato underlined with lettuce leaves on the other end of the platter. Oyster fork stuck in quarter of lemon on platter facing guest. Chilled tea plate for service. 2 packages crackers on tea plate.

OYSTERS, CREAM STEW: Six [6] oysters. Stew in their own juice until they curl, then pour hot cream and heat a short while, but do not let come to boil. Serve in soup tureen underlined with tureen plate with tureen ladle on plate. For service serve soup plate underlined with breakfast plate with soup ladle in soup plate, also dessert spoon. Crackers on tea plate.

OYSTERS, MILK STEW: Same as Oysters, Cream Stew, except substitute milk for cream. If oysters are small, chef should use discretion.

GRILLED SHAD ROE, BACON: Take contents of one 7½ oz. can of shad roe and brush roe with butter. Sprinkle with salt and pepper and broil in pan about 10 minutes, until thoroughly heated. Serve on breakfast plate with two slices of broiled bacon. Garnish with ¼ lemon and parsley.

BAKED FISH, CREOLE SAUCE: Use best fish market affords for baking. Dip in cooking oil; dust with paprika and bake in oven in roasting pan until done. Serve on hot medium platter with Creole Sauce poured over same. Garnish with parsley and 1/8 lemon. Breakfast plate for service. Table d'hôte: serve on breakfast plate. Garnish with sprig of parsley and 1/8 lemon.

CREOLE SAUCE:

1 clove
6 medium onions
6 green peppers
1 button garlic
2 #3 cans tomatoes
2 cups French or small peas
2 cups pimentos, 1" slices
2 cups mushrooms, sliced

PREPARATION: Sauté onions, peppers [sliced in 1 inch Julienne] and garlic about 5 minutes. Add tomatoes, mushrooms, simmer about 30 minutes. Finish with peas and pimentos.

SOUTHERN SHRIMP CREOLE:

1½ cups uncooked rice
6 outside branches celery, diced
3 medium onions, chopped
1 large green pepper, chopped
½ lb. fresh mushrooms, sliced
4 cups canned tomatoes
¼ cup pimientos, chopped
1 clove garlic, finely chopped
2 tablespoons flour
½ teaspoon black pepper
2 teaspoons salt
2 teaspoons chili powder
4 tablespoons butter or bacon fat
2 cups water
2 teaspoons sugar
1 tablespoon vinegar
2 lbs. fresh shrimp

Sauté celery, onions, green pepper and mushrooms slowly in butter or bacon fat for 10 minutes. Add flour and seasonings and mix well. Add tomatoes, pimientos and garlic. Add water slowly and simmer for about an hour or until thick, stirring constantly. Add fresh shrimp which have been previously cooked. Simmer about five minutes or until shrimp are thoroughly heated. Serve on a hot platter around a mound of fluffy rice. Serves six to eight portions.

To prepare fluffy boiled rice:

1½ cups rice
4 teaspoons salt
10 cups boiling water

Wash rice thoroughly; add salt to boiling water in deep saucepan. Add rice slowly so boiling does not stop. If water is very hard, add one teaspoon lemon juice or one tablespoon vinegar to keep rice white. Boil gently without stirring for 12 to 25 minutes, depending upon variety, or until rice is entirely soft when pressed between fingers. Drain into sieve, wash with hot water, cover with cloth, and set over hot water to separate grains.

To prepare green shrimp:

1 qt. boiling water	1 bay leaf
½ chopped onion	1 teaspoon black pepper
1 branch celery	½ lemon
2 teaspoons salt	

Cook these ingredients for 15 minutes in boiling water. Add shrimp and cook for 10 to 15 minutes. Let cool in broth. Remove shell and black sand vein.

<u>SPECIAL COLD PLATE</u>—Trains 37 and 38 only.

       Attach flyer to both luncheon and dinner menu.

             Tomato Juice—See Page 43

Take frozen green shrimp, 21 to 25 count to the pound, using a quart of boiling salted water for each pound of shrimp. Add 3 or 4 bay leaves to this water and when it comes to a brisk boil add the frozen shrimp. When the water again comes to a boil after the shrimp have been added, cook for 15 to 20 minutes, then let simmer for 5 minutes longer. Rinse in cold water. Peel and remove the black vein from the back of the shrimp and chill in ice water for about 30 minutes to make firm. Drain and dry thoroughly. Serve 6 to 8 shrimp according to size on a bed of shredded lettuce on breakfast plate which has been underlined with additional lettuce leaves, placing the shrimp in the center of the plate lengthwise. Garnish one side of the shrimp with ½ hard-boiled egg and ¼ wedge of lemon and on the other side with two slices of tomatoes. Pour one tablespoonful of Arnaud Sauce over the shrimp.

Serve two packages of flake crackers or ry-krisp on tea plate underlined with doily. Choice of beverage and dessert on menu Arnaud Sauce will come in quart bottles which you should order from the commissary. Shrimp will come in 5-1lb. boxes frozen.

SOUPS

<u>CHCIKEN BROTH, RICE:</u> Add boiled rice to one gallon of chicken broth which has been fortified with chicken concentrate, also a small amount of diced chicken. Serve in hot bouillon cup underlined with saucer. Sprinkle with chopped parsley just before serving. Bouillon spoon for service. Crackers on tea plate underlined with doily.

<u>COLD CONSOMME:</u> Use canned beef consommé, which should be chilled thoroughly in the can, when opened place in crock and store in chill box. Serve in a chilled bouillon cup underlined with saucer. Bouillon spoon on right side for service, on left side 1/8 lemon. Cracker on tea plate underlined with doily.

<u>CREAM OF CHICKEN SOUP:</u>

2 onions
½ cup chicken fat
1½ cups flour
3 stalks celery, sliced
1 gallon chicken stock

<u>PREPARATION:</u> Place vegetables in sauce pan, add lard and braise until soft. Then add 1½ cups flour and make a roux. Cook about 10 minutes, add 1 gallon boiling chicken stock, stir constantly, let simmer not less than 30 minutes, season with salt only, add 1 cup boiling cream, let come to boil once more, and strain into container. NOTE: To prevent crust from forming after soup is in container, place several small pieces of fat on top. Soup served in bouillon cup, underlined with saucer. Bouillon spoon for service. Crackers on tea plate underlined with doily.

<u>CREAM OF TOMATO SOUP:</u> Serve in bouillon cup underlined with saucer. Bouillon spoon for service. Crackers on tea plate underlined with doily.

1 veal or ham shank, and meat cut into small pieces
2 kitchenspoons* fat
2 cups celery, cut up

2 cups onions, cut up
2 cups carrots, cut up
1 cup flour
1 to 1½ cups cream
6 allspice
3 bay leaves
4 cans whole tomatoes
2 level kitchenspoons* sugar
1 gallon water
salt and pepper

PREPARATION: Place bones, meat, celery, onions, carrots, and paprika into sauce pan and sauté together with the 2 kitchenspoons fat until the onions begin to get soft, then add flour and make a roux. Let cook for 10 minutes, add water, tomatoes, spices, and sugar. Bring to boil, then simmer until meat is soft and puree reduced to 1½ gallons. Season with salt, pepper, strain, add 1½ cups boiling cream.

* 1 Kitchenspoon = 4 tablespoons

OLD FASHIONED NAVY BEAN SOUP:

2½ cups Navy beans—soaked overnight
1 gallon water
1 ham shank
2 cups canned tomatoes
¾ cup onions, cut in ¼ inch dice
1 cup celery, cut in ¼ inch dice
2 cups raw potatoes, cut in ¼ inch dice

PREPARATION: Place beans, all vegetables, including the tomatoes, and ham hock in sauce pan. Cover with 1 gallon water and cook until done. Remove ham hock, take out bones, remove surplus fat, and cut meat into ¼ inch dice. Add meat to soup and serve. Sprinkle with chopped parsley. Serve in bouillon cup underlined with saucer. Bouillon spoon for service. Crackers on tea plate underlined with doily.

ENGLISH BEEF BROTH: [Ingredients for one gallon]

1 kitchenspoon* shortening
1 cup celery, cut in ¼ inch dice
1 cup turnips, cut in ¼ inch dice
2 cups carrots, cut in ¼ inch dice
2 cups onions, cut in ¼ inch dice
1 gallon consommé
1 cup cooked lean beef [use small loin trimmings]
1 kitchenspoon* parsley, chopped and washed

PREPARATION: Place shortening in sauce pan, melt, add vegetables, and sauté for 5 minutes. Add consommé and cook slowly until vegetables are done. Finally, add meat and parsley, season with salt and pepper and teaspoon of Worcestershire Sauce. Serve in bouillon cup underlined with saucer. Bouillon spoon for service. Crackers on tea plate underlined with doily.

* 1 Kitchenspoon = 4 tablespoons

HOT CONSOMME: Use canned consommé. Keep hot in crock on steam table. Serve in bouillon cup underlined with saucer. Bouillon spoon for service. Crackers on tea plate underlined with doily.

JELLIED CONSOMME MADRILENE: Use canned consommé madrilène, which should be chilled thoroughly in the can, then opened, placed in a crock and stored in chill box. Serve in chilled bouillon cup underlined with saucer. Bouillon spoon on right side for service. On left side 1/8 lemon. Crackers on tea plate underlined with doily.

ONION SOUP AU GRATIN: Add contents of one 8-ounce jar of onion soup mix to 5 quarts of boiling water and let simmer for twenty-five minutes. Place piece of rye toast, cut round with biscuit cutter and covered with grated Parmesan or Roman Cheese, in bottom of bouillon cup and fill with onion soup, underline with saucer, bouillon spoon for service. Crackers on tea plate underlined with doily.

ONION SOUP—PARMESAN: Same as Onion Soup Au Gratin

PUREE OF SPLIT PEA SOUP: [Ingredients for 1½ gallons]

½ ham hock
2 onions
2 carrots
1 bay leaf
½ cup flour
½ kitchenspoon fat [2 tablespoons]
2 lbs. green split peas
3 outside celery
3 whole allspice
1¾ gallons stock [beef, veal, or chicken]

PREPARATION: Place the chopped up ham hock in a large sauce pan with the fat, and braise a few minutes. Then add whole onions, carrots, celery, and spice; simmer for 5 minutes longer. Add peas, mix well, add flour, mix again, and add stock. Season and cook until done and soup is reduced to 1½ gallons. Strain. Serve in bouillon cup underlined with saucer, bouillon spoon for service. Crackers on tea plate underlined with doily.

VEGETABLE SOUP: [Ingredients for 1 gallon]

2 onions, sliced
2 carrots, sliced
3 white turnips
1 #2½ can tomatoes
4 pieces outside celery, sliced
1½ gallons stock [beef, veal, or chicken]
1 tablespoon chopped, washed parsley

PREPARATION: Grease bottom of sauce pan with a little fat. Add vegetables. Add stock and tomatoes. Cook until vegetables are done and soup is reduced to 1 gallon. Season to taste and then add the chopped parsley. If fresh peas, string beans, or lima beans are on car, add some to soup. Serve in bouillon cup underlined with saucer. Bouillon spoon for service. Crackers on tea plate underlined with doily.

CHICKEN GUMBO SOUP: [Ingredients for 2 gallons]

2 kitchenspoons* melted butter
1 onion, chopped fine
3 green peppers, cut in ¼ inch dice and blanched
1 cup washed raw rice, boiled in salted water
1½ gallons chicken stock
1 No. 2½ can tomatoes, chopped fine
2 No. 2 cans cut okra
1 cup celery, cut in ¼ inch dice
Fortify with chicken concentrate

PREPARATION: Sauté onions, peppers, and celery together in melted butter until onions are soft. Add stock and tomatoes and let cook until rice is well done. Add okra and let come to boil. Season with salt and pepper and add cup diced chicken. Serve in bouillon cup underlined with saucer. Crackers on tea plate underlined with doily. Bouillon spoon for service.

*1 kitchenspoon = 4 tablespoons

GREEN PEA SOUP: Use Liptons Green Pea Soup Mix, following directions on the can. Serve in bouillon cup underlined with saucer, bouillon spoon for service. Individual package of crackers on tea plate underlined with doily.

The page with the Green Pea Soup was revised and corrected on March 12, 1957. The railroad was already aware of rising costs and, if a canned product was of suitable quality, it would be used as opposed to cooking from scratch.

VEGETABLES

BEETS IN BUTTER: Use canned beets. Heat in sauce pan, slice, season with salt and pepper and butter. Serve in fruit saucer. On Table d'hôte, serve in small baker.

BLACKEYED PEAS: 2 pounds blackeyed peas. Wash thoroughly and soak overnight. Put in sauce pan and add 2 quarts cold water and ½ pound salt pork diced, heat to boiling point and simmer until peas and salt pork are tender. Salt to taste and serve in fruit saucer. On Table d'hôte, serve in small baker.

BOILED ONIONS IN CREAM: Use small silver skin onions. Peel and wash carefully; boil in cold salted water with a little milk added to keep onions white. Cook until done. Serve 4 or 5 onions with cream sauce in fruit saucer. Serve in small baker, Table d'hôte.

CREAM SAUCE: [Ingredients for ½ gallon]

½ cup butter or chicken fat
1½ quarts boiling milk
1 cup flour
Salt

PREPARATION: Melt butter or chicken fat in sauce pan. Add flour and make a roux. Let cook at least 10 minutes to which add boiling milk gradually, stirring constantly with egg whip to prevent sauce getting lumpy. Cook 30 minutes. Season with salt only. Strain into crock and place small bits of butter on top to prevent crust forming.

BOILED POTATOES, PARSLEY BUTTER: Select potatoes of uniform size, wash thoroughly and boil by dropping into cold water in a sauce pan. Add sufficient salt. Vessel to be covered and potatoes boiled until done. Drain off water. Set back on range to dry and steam for few minutes. Serve in fruit saucer, with butter sauce. Sprinkle with chopped parsley before serving. Serve in small baker, Table d'hôte.

BOILED WHITE ONIONS IN BUTTER: Use small silver skin onions. Peel and wash carefully; boil in cold salted water with a little milk added to keep onions white. Cook until done. Serve 4 or 5 onions with butter sauce in fruit saucer. Serve in small baker, Table d'hôte.

BRAISED CELERY:
3 bunches celery
1 onion, peeled and sliced
1 carrot, pared and sliced
1 sprig parsley
2 tablespoons butter
1 teaspoon salt
few grains pepper
1 cup consommé

Wash celery and remove top leaves. Cut each celery head lengthwise through heart, making six pieces. Cut pieces in half if necessary. Arrange the onions and carrots with the parsley in the bottom of the pan. Lay the celery on top, dot with butter, and sprinkle with the salt and pepper. Add consommé, cover, and bake in a moderately hot oven for 1 hour. Serve in fruit saucer. Serve in small baker, Table d'hôte.

BUTTERED CARROTS: Wash, pare, slice, and cook in salted water until tender. Drain, pour melted butter over. Serve in fruit saucer. Serve in small baker, Table d'hôte.

CORN O'BRIEN: Sauté onions and diced green peppers in butter until soft, do not brown. Add canned whole kernel corn and heat well. The last few minutes add chopped pimentos. Mix well and serve in fruit saucer. Serve in small baker, Table D'hôte.

COLE SLAW: Shred raw cabbage cutting out the heart or core, which must not be used. Place in crock. Take 1 cup mayonnaise, cut with 1/3 cup vinegar, stirring as vinegar is added. Season with salt, pepper, and a little sugar to taste. Pour this over the shredded cabbage and let set about 1 hour before serving in chill box. Serve liberal portion in fruit saucer, Table D'hôte. Serve in oatmeal bowl, A La Carte. Top with julienned carrots just before serving.

BOILED CABBAGE: Take off outside leaves and cut head into ¼, 1/6, or 1/8 depending on size of head. Remove the tough core. Cook uncovered in salted boiling water for 15 to 20 minutes. Drain, chop, and serve liberal portion in fruit saucer.

COLLARD GREENS: Use canned collard greens, season with chopped diced ham and serve in fruit saucer. Use hock and ends of ham for this. Serve in small baker, Table d'hôte.

ESCALLOPED POTATOES:

5 medium sized potatoes
4 tablespoons butter
salt and pepper
2 tablespoons flour
milk

PREPARATION: Pare raw potatoes and cut them into thin slices. Place in baking pan a layer of potatoes 1 inch deep, season with salt and pepper, sprinkle a portion of the flour over each layer. Add a part of the butter in bits. Then add another layer of potatoes and seasoning as before, and continue until the required amount is used. It is advisable not to have more than 2 or 3 layers because of the difficulty in cooking. Add milk until it can be seen between the slices of potatoes, cover and bake until potatoes are tender when pierced with a fork. Remove the cover during the last 15 minutes to brown the top. Serve from baking pan in fruit saucer. Serve in small baker, Table d'hôte.

FLAKED POTATOES: Cut peeled potatoes into pieces. Cover with cold water, add salt, and cook until done. Drain well, set pot back on range, and steam until dry. Force through potato ricer into mixing bowl; add butter and boiling hot milk. Stir and heat well until light and fluffy. Serve in fruit saucer. Serve in small baker, Table d'hôte.

FRENCH FRIED EGG PLANT: Peel and cut egg plant into slices ½ inch thick and 2 inches long. Salt, pepper, roll in Redi-Breader. Fry in deep fat. When done, remove to clean towel to absorb excess grease. Serve 5 pieces in fruit saucer. Serve 3 pieces in small baker, Table d'hôte.

FRENCH FRIED ONION RINGS: Onions should be sliced and then separated into rings, all except the small center rings should be dipped into egg wash, then into flour, and fried a nice brown. Little center rings can be used in potato salad, soups, etc. A La Carte, serve on small platter.

FRIED POTATOES: Take boiled potatoes, slice and fry until brown. Serve a liberal portion on small platter.

FRIED SWEET POTATOES: Wash, boil, and peel potatoes. Cut into slices. Fry in hot grease, and serve in fruit saucer. Serve in small baker, Table d'hôte.

GREEN ASPARAGUS, DRAWN BUTTER: Serve 6 or 8 spears, according to size in individual celery tray, drawn butter poured over same.
PREPARATION: We will use fresh asparagus as long as it is in season and available. It should be prepared as follows: Asparagus should be scraped and the tough part of the stalk removed. Then tie in bunches with white cotton cord and cook until tender in boiling salted water. When fresh asparagus is not available, we will use frozen asparagus spears. They should be prepared by cooking in boiling, salted water until tender.

GREEN BEANS: Cut ends of each bean and be sure every shred of string is removed. Wash well, do not break or cut in half unless extremely large and long. Cook in boiling salted water. In preparing green beans, you will take a small piece of salt pork and boil it until about 2/3 done, then put it in the green beans. This will remove some of the salt and grease and give the beans an excellent flavor. Serve in fruit saucer. Serve in small baker, Table d'hôte.

GREEN LIMA BEANS: When frozen lima beans are used, cook piece of salt pork in boiling water until 2/3 done. Add beans to water and cook until done. Drain carefully and add a little pepper. Serve in fruit saucer. Serve in small baker, Table d'hôte. When canned lima beans are used, add a little bacon grease and heat. Season with a small amount of salt and pepper. Serve in fruit saucer. Serve in small baker, Table d'hôte.

GREEN PEAS: Use frozen peas. Cook in boiling water [salted] about 20 minutes until done. Drain and season with salt and butter. Serve in fruit saucer. Serve in small baker, Table d'hôte. Canned green peas may be substituted.

GARDEN SPINACH: Use canned spinach. Heat and serve in fruit saucer. Serve in small baker, Table d'hôte.

HARVARD BEETS:

1 cup sugar
1 teaspoon salt
4 tablespoon butter or fat
3 tablespoons corn starch
1½ cups vinegar

PREPARATION: Mix sugar, corn starch and salt. Add vinegar and let the sauce boil for 5 minutes, stirring constantly. Add fat. Pour the sauce over the beets and let stand for a few minutes to absorb the sweet-sour flavor of the sauce. The above recipe should be able to take care of 6 #2 cans of beets. The beets should be sliced thin for this service. Serve liberal amount in fruit saucer. Table d'hôte, serve in small baker.
NOTE: On light lines, recipes should be cut in half or fourth according to amount of business done. Sauce should be made fresh daily.

MASHED POTATOES: Cut peeled potatoes into even sized pieces, cover with cold water, add salt and cook, covered until done. Drain well, set pot back on range and let steam until dry. Force through potato ricer into mixing bowl, add boiling milk. Stir and beat well until light and fluffy. Serve in fruit saucer. Serve in small baker, Table d'hôte. [WHERE CARS ARE SUPPLIED WITH INSTANT OR INSTANT FLAKE POTATOES YOU ARE TO FOLLOW THE DIRECTIONS ON THE CAN OR PACKAGE IN THE PREPARATION OF THESE ITEMS].

MASHED SWEET POTATOES: Take sweet potatoes and parboil until done, then peel them. Put in sauce pan and season with butter, salt, and sugar and then whip until fluffy. Serve in fruit saucer. Serve in small baker, Table d'hôte.

NEW CORN IN BUTTER: Use frozen corn. Boil until done, drain, then sauté in butter. Season with salt and pepper and add a little bacon grease. Serve in fruit saucer. Serve in small baker, Table d'hôte. Note: You can back up frozen corn with #2 can of whole kernel corn.

NEW POTATOES IN CREAM: Use small or medium boiled new potatoes, 2 or 3. Place in fruit saucer with cream sauce poured over. Place in small baker, Table d'hôte.

CREAM SAUCE: [Ingredients for ½ gallon]

½ cup butter or chicken fat
1½ quarts boiling milk
1 cup flour
Salt

PREPARATION: Melt butter or chicken fat in sauce pan. Add flour and make a roux. Let cook at least 10 minutes to which add boiling milk gradually, stirring constantly with egg whip to prevent sauce getting lumpy. Cook 30 minutes. Season with salt only. Strain into crock and place small bits of butter on top to prevent crust forming.

NEW POTATOES, PARSLEY BUTTER: Use small or medium boiled new potatoes, 2 or 3 to be served in fruit saucer with butter sauce. Sprinkle with chopped parsley. Serve in small baker, Table d'hôte.

SLICED TOMATOES, SOUTHERN: Serve 3 slices of tomato overlapping each other on lettuce leaves on tea plate. Liberal portion of Durkee's dressing poured over.

BROCCOLI, LEMON BUTTER SAUCE: Bring to boil four [4] cups of water, add two [2] bastingspoons of bacon grease or grease from salt pork. Then add one, two-pound box of frozen broccoli, cook 17 minutes. If broccoli is not frozen, cook 12 minutes. Only cook a small amount of broccoli at a time. COOKS WILL SAVE THE GREASE FROM BREAKFAST BACON AND SALT PORK FOR THIS PURPOSE. Serve in individual celery trough; sprinkle with lemon butter sauce.

LEMON BUTTER SAUCE: Melt ½ pound butter and add juice of one lemon.

STEWED TOMATOES WITH OKRA: Use 2/3 amount tomatoes to 1/3 amount of okra. Season with salt and pepper and a little butter. Use canned tomatoes and okra. Serve in fruit saucer. Serve in small baker, Table d'hôte.

SUCCOTASH: Use canned cream style corn and lima beans. The corn and lima beans mixed together. 1/3 corn and 2/3 lima beans. Season with salt, pepper, and butter. Add a small amount of bacon grease for seasoning. Serve in fruit saucer. Serve in small baker, Table d'hôte.

SWEET POTATOES, CANDIED: Boil the potatoes in their skin. Peel and cut in halves, lengthwise. Make a syrup of sugar, water, and butter. Use juice of lemon. Place potatoes in baking pan. Pour syrup over potatoes and place in oven. Baste potatoes with syrup from time to time. Syrup left in pan to be poured over potatoes when served. Serve hot in fruit saucer. Serve in small baker, Table d'hôte.

SWEET POTATOES, HAWAIIAN: Take sweet potatoes and parboil until done, then peel them. Put in sauce pan and season with butter, salt, and sugar, and a little lemon juice. Add liberal amount of crushed pineapple and whip until fluffy. Serve in fruit saucer. Serve in small baker, Table d'hôte.

SWEET POTATOES, MARSHMALLOW: Take sweet potatoes and parboil until done, then peel them. Put in sauce pan and season with butter, salt, and sugar and then whip until fluffy. Pile lightly in shallow baking pan, top with marshmallows and just before serving place in oven and brown marshmallows. Serve in fruit saucer. Serve in small baker, Table d'hôte.

SWEET POTATOES, SOUTHERN: Boil the potatoes in their skin. Peel and cut in halves, lengthwise. Make a syrup of sugar, water, and butter. Use juice of lemon. Place potatoes in baking pan. Pour syrup over potatoes and place in oven. Baste potatoes with syrup from time to time. Syrup left in pan to be poured over potatoes when served. Serve in fruit saucer. Serve in small baker, Table d'hôte.

SWEET POTATOES AND APPLES, SOUTHERN: Boil the potatoes in their skin. Peel and cut in halves, lengthwise. Make a syrup of sugar, water, and butter. Use juice of lemon. Place potatoes and canned apples in baking pan. Pour syrup over potatoes and apples and place in oven. Baste with syrup from time to time. Syrup left in pan to be poured over potatoes and apples when served. Serve hot in fruit saucer. Serve in small baker, Table d'hôte.

TINY BEETS, HARVARD:

1 cup of sugar
1 teaspoon salt
4 tablespoons butter or fat
3 tablespoons of corn starch
1½ cups vinegar

PREPARATION: Mix sugar, corn starch and salt. Add vinegar and let the sauce boil for 5 minutes, stirring constantly. Add fat. Pour the sauce over the beets and let stand for a few minutes to absorb the sweet-sour flavor of the sauce. The above recipe should be ample to take care of 6 #2 cans of beets. The beets should be sliced thin for this service. Serve liberal amount in fruit saucer. Serve in small baker, Table d'hôte.

TURNIP GREENS: Use #2 or #10 can turnip greens. First boil small piece of salt pork until about 2/3 done to get the salt and grease out, then season turnip greens with the salt pork. Serve in fruit saucer. Serve in small baker, Table d'hôte.

TURNIP GREENS, PEPERONCINI: Use #2 or #10 can turnip greens. First boil small piece of salt pork until about 2/3 done to get the salt and grease out, then season turnip greens with the salt pork. Peperoncini [sweet pickle peppers] will be furnished in quart jars— place one whole peperoncini pepper on top of turnip greens from the jar [do not heat the pepper]. Serve in fruit saucer. Serve in small baker, Table d'hôte.

MUSTARD GREENS: Use #2 can mustard greens. First boil small piece of salt pork until about 2/3 done to get the salt and grease out, then season mustard greens with the salt pork. Serve in fruit saucer. Serve in small baker, Table d'hôte.

WHIPPED POTATOES: Cut peeled potatoes into pieces, cover with cold water, add salt and cook until done. Drain well, set pot back on range, and steam until dry. Force through potato ricer into mixing bowl, add butter and boiling milk. Stir and beat until light and fluffy. Serve in fruit saucer. Serve in small baker, Table d'hôte.

NAVY BEANS:

2 pounds navy beans
2 teaspoons salt
2½ quarts cold water
4 teaspoons sugar
dash of pepper
½ pound salt pork, diced

Pick over and wash beans thoroughly in cold water. Let beans soak overnight. Place beans in sauce pan, add remaining ingredients, cover and simmer until beans are tender but not mushy. Shake the pan occasionally to prevent beans sticking. Serve in fruit saucer. Serve in small baker, Table d'hôte.

VEGETABLE PLATE, POACHED EGG: Serve five different vegetables on dinner plate, each vegetable separated by a strip of toast, with a poached egg resting on a round piece of toast in center. Garnish with parsley.

STEWED SUMMER SQUASH: Wash thoroughly and cut in half inch, crosswise slices, without removing the skin. Place in sauce pan and add enough boiling water so it can just be seen through the top layer, not enough to cover. Add salt, allowing about ¼ teaspoon for each pound of squash. Cover pan and cook moderately fast until tender, about six minutes for young squash. Shake pan from time to time to prevent sticking. Remove cover and season with butter and dash of pepper. Serve in fruit saucer. Serve in small baker, Table d'hôte.

TINY WHOLE BEETS IN BUTTER: Use canned tiny whole beets. Heat in sauce pan, season with salt, pepper, and butter. Serve in fruit saucer. Serve in small baker, Table d'hôte.

ESCALLOPED TOMATOES: Drain into bowl juice from canned tomatoes. Butter a baking pan, cover bottom with layer of tomatoes, add bits of butter, season with salt and pepper and sprinkle with fresh bread crumbs. Then repeat with tomatoes, seasoning, and crumbs, in order, until pan is full. Add tomato juice, sprinkle some crumbs on top, and bake in oven for 20 minutes. Serve in fruit saucer. Serve in small baker, Table d'hôte.

HASHED BROWNED POTATOES: Take boiled potatoes, hash and fry until brown. Serve a liberal portion on small platter. On Table d'hôte serve in small baker.

DICED POTATOES IN CREAM: Wash, peel, and dice potatoes. Boil until done. Serve in fruit saucer with cream sauce poured over. Serve in small baker, Table d'hôte.

CREAM SAUCE: [Ingredients for ½ gallon]

½ cup butter or chicken fat
1½ quarts boiling milk
1 cup flour
Salt

PREPARATION: Melt butter or chicken fat in sauce pan. Add flour and make a roux. Let cook at least 10 minutes to which add boiling milk gradually, stirring constantly with egg whip to prevent sauce getting lumpy. Cook 30 minutes. Season with salt only. Strain into crock and place small bits of butter on top to prevent crust forming.

STEAMED BRUSSELS SPROUTS: Bring to boil 2½ cups water, add 2 bastingspoons of bacon grease or grease from salt pork. Then add one 2½ pound box of frozen Brussels sprouts, cook 10 to 12 minutes. If Brussels sprouts are not frozen cook 5 to 7 minutes. Only cook a small amount of Brussels sprouts at a time, being careful not to overcook. COOKS WILL SAVE THE GREASE FROM BREAKFAST BACON AND SALT PORK FOR THIS PURPOSE. Serve in fruit saucer. Serve in small baker, Table d'hôte.

MIXED GARDEN GREENS: Use #2 can turnip greens and kale. Mix equal parts of each. First boil small piece of salt pork until about 2/3 done to get the salt and grease out. Then season the mixed greens with the salt pork. Serve in fruit saucer. Serve in small baker, Table d'hôte.

FRESH STEWED CORN: Cut corn from cob using very sharp knife and cutting off only about ½ depth of kernels. After cutting all around ear, use back of knife to scrape out remaining juice and pulp, scraping down only—not back and forth. Use one cup water for each three cups of corn. Cover and simmer gently for ten minutes or until tender. Add one cup of milk and two tablespoons of bacon drippings to the above corn and simmer ten minutes longer. Season to taste with salt and pepper. Serve in fruit saucer. Serve in small baker, Table d'hôte.

CAULIFLOWER, CREAM SAUCE: Soak fresh cauliflower in enough cold water to cover for about one-half hour. Drain, wash head and trim by cutting off base of stalk and discarding all large leaves. The tiny leaves that cling to the outer floweret may be left on. Break flowerets apart, removing large main stem. Drop into a generous amount of boiling salted water and cook rapidly until tender, about 6 to 8 minutes. Test by piercing with fork [do not overcook]. Drain thoroughly and serve liberal amount in fruit saucer with cream sauce poured over for A La Carte. Table d'hôte, serve in small baker. Use frozen cauliflower if fresh not available, but do not soak or trim as outlined above. COOK ONLY A SMALL AMOUNT OF CAULIFLOWER AT A TIME.

CREAM SAUCE: [Ingredients for ½ gallon]

½ cup butter or chicken fat
1½ quarts boiling milk
1 cup flour
Salt

PREPARATION: Melt butter or chicken fat in sauce pan. Add flour and make a roux. Let cook at least 10 minutes to which add boiling milk gradually, stirring constantly with egg whip to prevent sauce getting lumpy. Cook 30 minutes. Season with salt only. Strain into crock and place small bits of butter on top to prevent crust forming.

Made in the USA
Charleston, SC
06 July 2013